BREAKING THE FRAME

FILM LANGUAGE AND THE EXPERIENCE OF LIMITS

INEZ HEDGES

INDIANA UNIVERSITY PRESS
Bloomington and Indianapolis

The paper used in this publication meets the minimum requirements of American
National Standard for Information Sciences—Permanence of Paper for Printed
Library Materials, ANSI Z39.48-1984.

♾ ™

Manufactured in the United States of America

Library of Congress Cataloging-in-Publication Data

Hedges, Inez, date.
  Breaking the frame : film language and the experience of limits /
Inez Hedges.
    p. cm.
  Includes bibliographical references and index.
  ISBN 0-253-32722-9 (cloth). — ISBN 0-253-20621-9 (paper)
  1. Motion pictures—Philosophy. 2. Motion pictures and
literature. I. Title.
PN1995.H398 1991
791.43′01—dc20   90-38728
                                                            CIP

1 2 3 4 5 95 94 93 92 91

For Janice and Irwin Hedges

CONTENTS

ILLUSTRATIONS

Acknowledgments

During the time I have been working on this project, my colleagues at North-eastern University have provided unfailing support. I wish to thank the University Council on Research and Scholarship for several awards, including a junior sabbatical and summer grant, that enabled me to complete the project. The chairman of the Department of Modern Languages, Holbrook C. Robinson, is responsible for the pleasant and productive atmosphere that has prevailed there for many years. Michael Lipton, chairman of the Department of Philosophy, gave computer assistance with a great deal of patience.

The United States Fulbright Commission provided the research sabbatical that enabled me to work at the Raymond Queneau archives in Verviers, Belgium. Many thanks to the Curator, André Blavier, for his enthusiasm and expert assistance, and to Odette Blavier for her wonderful friendship.

Several friends have read chapters of this book and made valuable suggestions. J. Dudley Andrew generously offered his comments after I read a first version of the Truffaut chapter at a meeting for the Society for Cinema Studies. John Bernstein was present at the project's inception, and I am grateful for both his encouragement and his insightful remarks. My colleague Sam Bishop interrupted his sabbatical to read the typescript and to make valuable suggestions. Stanley Cavell's film seminar provided me with a stimulating environment for developing my thoughts and offered the chance to be a part of an ongoing conversation about film. Jean Decock has been a tireless editor at *The French Review* for many years and has offered me the opportunity to present a number of my ideas in article form. Miriam Hansen read several chapters and graciously shared her own work-in-progress with me. Stephen Heath has been a constant friend and example throughout.

Bridget Kinally made it possible to illustrate the book with stills from the collections of the British Film Institute and in addition provided a charming atmosphere in which to work. Beth Rhoades at the Philadelphia Museum of Art and Thomas D. Grischkowsky at the Museum of Modern Art, New York, supplied reproductions from their collections. Maria Pérez Andújar obtained the reproduction of *Las Meninas*, graciously provided by the Museo del Prado, during her trip to Madrid. To all, many thanks.

My special gratitude goes to my husband, Victor Wallis, whose willingness to participate in the final revision turned the project into a special kind of sharing.

I would like to thank the editors of the following journals for permission to reprint excerpts from earlier articles: *Journal of Contemporary History* and *Substance*. An earlier version of chapter 2 appeared in *Bucknell Review*, 32:1. Chapter 8 originally appeared in *L'Esprit créateur* 26:4 and chapter 1 in *The French Review* 58:2. These have all been substantially revised for the present volume.

Introduction

In the 60s it was commonplace to say that the cinema had replaced the novel as the popular narrative art form. Today, the cinema itself, as an institution defined by a particular distribution and exhibition system, is on the decline. The social practice of "going to the movies" is being edged out by home consumption. This erosion of the social is in many ways regrettable. In particular, the shrinking of the movie audience has meant that studios have placed increasing emphasis on "blockbuster" films that look more and more alike every year. But there have been pluses as well. The widespread distribution and availability of films on videotape has radically changed their audience. Films can now be checked out of tape libraries like books, perused, studied, and viewed at leisure. As viewers we are in a position to fill in the gaps of our film literacy. Better still, we can go back and check our hunches and interpretations by seeing the films again.

The critic who writes about film now does so for a much wider audience. Since the experience of films is no longer limited to their short runs in movie theaters or occasional revivals in art houses, they have increasingly become the subject of discussions and private reflections among the general public. This has meant a growth in the readership of books about film as well. Along with historical studies or production stories, books that deal with broader cultural issues (such as Bill Nichols's *Ideology and the Image* and Teresa de Lauretis's *Alice Doesn't*) have been especially well received. The idea that cinematic works have served as the medium of expression for some of the most important philosophical and humanist concerns of our time is by now widely accepted.

In the chapters that follow I have attempted to set down some of my own thoughts about the way films have spoken to major issues in contemporary criticism. The examples chosen come mainly from the French New Wave and after, although a few older Hollywood films are included. Naturally, I cannot claim to be exhaustive in content, or even to have developed a "system" for analyzing film. Instead, I have tried to remain open to many avenues of reflection stimulated by recent writing in the fields of literary theory, psychoanalysis, philosophy, and feminist studies. This book is meant not only for scholars of film, but for the wider readership of today's "filmliterate" public who may enjoy exploring the theoretical and philosophical implications of films they have seen. It is meant to stimulate the imagination rather than cut off discussion by "authoritative" readings.

The common thread that unites these essays is a preoccupation with films that challenge accepted norms in both form and content. They literally break out of conventional frames—hence the title of this book. By this I mean that they upset our expectations about how films should look (the film frame) as well as how experience is to be organized in film (the psychological or cognitive frame).

In my discussions, I will often use the concept of the cognitive frame for the set of expectations that experienced viewers bring to their reading of a film. The frames we use in viewing films may either be derived from those we apply to real-world experience or may be specific to film conventions or film genres.[1]

As we look at a film, perception occurs on many levels. On the one hand, the medium itself has a certain relation to reality. Except in animated and abstract films, the movie image is a photographic rendering of objects that have existed in the real world. To some extent, schemas which apply to real-world perception carry over to the film image. Even narrative, or story-telling, is a way of structuring information that occurs in real life as well as in art.

On the other hand, a film spectator relies on his or her knowledge of other films when encountering a new work. The intertextual dimension of film can account for expectations about genre, authorial style, and language. Most spectators will walk into a movie theater already expecting a certain *type* of film. Film studios are well aware of the way that the familiar attributes of a genre can reassure a film audience, and they are adept at repeating the familiar themes of westerns in such films as *Star Wars*, or at reviving old forms such as the *film noir* in *Prizzi's Honor*. In fact, the more original the world created by the film of fiction, the more conventional elements it must have in order to help the audience understand and enjoy it. As cognitive scientists have shown, people can't cope with too much new information all at once.

In addition to large-scale genre classifications, film spectators use their knowledge of filmmaking conventions to construct a mental representation of such elements of the fictional world as its story time and space, or such emotional mind sets as suspenseful expectation, fear, sorrow, or romantic wish-fulfillment. Emotion a spectator feels while watching a film can be induced by music, by editing, or by devices of framing or shooting that serve to guide those reactions. For instance, in *Citizen Kane* low-angle shots are frequently used to portray, from the subjective point of view of one character, the threat posed by another. Kane appears to Susan Alexander in this way when he orders her to continue her singing career, as does the politician Gettys to Kane when he corners Kane in Susan's apartment. Within the system of this film, then, low-angle shots are often used to connote one person's power over another. These same shots carry even more intertextual significance when juxtaposed with the visual themes of German expressionism, however. For spectators familiar with expressionism, the looming low-angle figures convey an additional connotation of power allied with evil. Thus those viewers who are more visually "literate" will have a more complex experience while watching the film than those who are not aware of these historical associations.

In works of art, the point is often to present new insights to the perceiver and to break away from what is expected. The impression of newness may be intended by the artist to influence the spectator in some carefully planned fashion. If we imagine a mental construct as a "frame," then the presentation of novel material that encourages the perceiver to modify those constructs may be seen as a kind of "frame-breaking." Whatever its form, frame-breaking goes against the expectation of the perceiver. The concept of "frames" provides a schema within which one can begin to explain the shifts in perception that many art works seek to achieve.

Our perception of reality is conditioned by the language we use. Benjamin Whorf, in *Language, Thought, and Reality*, first published in 1956, showed that thinking is "in a language"; the language that we think in subtly controls the patterns of our thoughts.[2] Some of his most impressive examples have to do with the way notions of time are expressed in language. For the Hopi culture, for instance, time is not motion in space (as it is for us) but a "getting later" of everything that has ever happened. The idea of "saving time" is meaningless in the context of that culture.[3] More recently, George Lakoff and Mark Johnson, in *Metaphors We Live By*, posit that "the most fundamental values in a culture will be coherent with the metaphorical structure of the most fundamental concepts in a culture." Their study focuses on so-called dead metaphors which form the basis for our speech—we are not even aware of the metaphors concealed in most of the expressions they analyze. For instance, they cite numerous examples to show that time is seen in our culture either as a moving object ("The time will come when . . . ") or as something stationary that we move through ("As we move into the 21st Century . . . ").[4]

The term "film language" has come to designate the conventions according to which cinematic works are made in such a way that their audiences can comprehend them. Like the spoken or written language described by linguists, the visual language of film exercises limitations as well as offering possibilities for expression. The style of editing developed in Hollywood in the 30s and 40s and which came to be known as "seamless" editing brought with it subtle forces of control. For example, the concept of a cohesive narrative space for the purpose of telling a story left out whatever reality might lie beyond that space— the cameras filming it, for one. In addition, the medium of cinema has not been immune to the suspicion of language that has characterized the latter half of our century—the desire to move outside of its "thought control." The first section focuses on some of the ways that filmmakers have raised these issues in their films.

Conventions of representation in a society (including those that govern a concept like "realism") are as culturally conditioned as conventions of language. The two chapters in the second section take up the question of the artist's relation to the cinema as an art of representation and the issue of changing frames of representation in different historical epochs.

"Seamless editing" was considered by its practitioners to be a form of realism: the idea was to avoid distracting the audience from the story by calling attention to the film apparatus. But the question of what constitutes cinematic realism has been a contested one in film. The French critic André Bazin wrote that the objective nature of photography forces us to "accept as real the existence of the object reproduced, actually re-presented, set before us, that is to say, in time and space."[5] Bazin argues that the cinema mummifies the past, preserves things by fixing the image of their duration. The idea that film can somehow reproduce objective reality separately from the subjective consciousness of the artist is no longer accepted today. A camera, after all, always films from somewhere, always leaves out more of the world than it can fit in. The selectivity involved in the editing process is a further manipulation of the image.

Even if we grant that the reality shown on film is subtly altered, how effective is the cinema in representing subjective states of mind? Some of the earliest writers on film held that the photographic image was limited to reproducing the surfaces of things. Yet the experience of German expressionism and French surrealism, which gave rise to important cinematic works in the 20s, argues against this view. In both cases, the film medium proved very effective in expressing inner reality. Expressionism modeled the external world into a representation of inner states of mind; surrealism operated a transformation of reality by a juxtaposition of images that reflected the logic of a dream. In the third section, I show that even mainstream narrative films have ways of showing the inner thoughts of the characters. Despite this, the portrayal of the inner lives of women characters remains a relatively rare occurrence in film. The films discussed are ones that achieve this, either through a sophisticated use of narrators or by letting us get to know the character by showing how she relates to the space surrounding her.

In the final section, I discuss how the film spectator is addressed by cinematic works in ways that are gender-specific. There is no more important aspect of a person's relation to reality than his or her conception of self as a gendered self. Most films reinforce received definitions of masculinity and femininity. Children's films, I argue, are among the most conservative; in contradistinction to many of the films discussed in the first three sections, it is hard to find films made for children that "break the frame" of received attitudes toward gender. No matter that women have made significant progress in the workplace in the latter half of the twentieth century; children's films still shy away from making a girl the central, active character. Or if they do, they still represent her in roles that exemplify all the negative characteristics of "femininity": passivity, fragility, and subservience to the male sex. The final chapter expands the argument to show how these problems are exacerbated in the film "star," who becomes the repository as well as the motor force for the machinery of sexual politics in the cinema. In the conclusion I offer some suggestions for a frame-breaking cinema that would constructively address the question of gender. By approaching the question of gender in a more thoughtful way, such films would creatively engage the spectator in a process of transformation. Ultimately, this would bring about new expressions of film language, representation, and subjectivity.

PART ONE

LANGUAGE

Not been
writtup

Spoken or written language is a system of conventions that allows us to communicate. Communication is most direct and effective when simple facts are being transmitted and grows progressively more complex with the addition of connotation, irony, and metaphor. Comparison among languages suggests, moreover, that even factual content is culture-bound rather than "objective." Semiotics has taught us that the association between a sound and the object or idea it denotes is arbitrary; comparative linguistics has shown that the cognitive map of each culture divides up reality in somewhat arbitrary chunks as well. Finally, historical experience has provided the lesson that societies can mean very different things by the same word.

The persistent habit of filmmakers of adapting novels and short stories to the screen tacitly asserts some equivalence between the languages of literature and cinema. Such adaptation must, however, always be a "translation": the modes of constructing time and space, encouraging identification, and organizing point of view in cinema require specific material supports that are not always shared by literature.

Narrative films resemble novels because of the way they are perceived: from visual and auditory information presented in successive moments of screen time, the perceiver constructs the diegetic space and time of the narrative. In addition, the mode of presentation resembles that of the novel: information about the time, place, and characters of a story is mediated by a narrator or narrators. The relationship among the above elements (where concepts such as omniscience, point of view, and reliability come into play) can be every bit as nuanced as in literature. The important sources in this area are Wayne C. Booth's *The Rhetoric of Fiction*, Mieke Bal's *Narratology*, and Seymour Chatman's *Story and Discourse*.

Unlike literature, film conveys information to the spectator on multiple channels: image, dialogue, music, sound effects. I use the term "arranger" for the controlling consciousness that must ultimately be held responsible for the selection and combination of the sounds and images of the film. The arranger should be distinguished from the film narrator, who is bound up with the point of view and can therefore usually be identified with the camera. I don't mean to suggest that the arranger of film is similar to the arranger, say, of music (someone who takes an original piece and modifies it); rather, I am borrowing this term from David Hayman, who first proposed it (in *Ulysses: The Mechanics of Meaning*) to account for the unifying narrative consciousness of James Joyce's *Ulysses*, a novel whose chapters are written in many different styles. Similarly, a film composes many different elements into its message. If, as often happens, its sound track and image track function equally as sources of new information, the concept of narrator is simply not nuanced enough to account for this complexity.

Like literature, film has the ability to distinguish between levels of narration. Some information may clearly be external to the story, in the sense that the characters living the represented fiction could not be aware of it. This information is called "extradiegetic." Examples would include extradiegetic music (sometimes called "mood" music); comments on the sound track in "voice-over" made by someone standing outside the story; or images inserted by the arranger that have no relation to the diegetic space. All of these are included solely for the purpose of influencing the perceptions of the film spectator.

Information known to only one character in the story is called "metadiegetic." The terms "extradiegetic" and "metadiegetic" are taken from Gérard Genette's *Narrative Discourse: An Essay in Method.* Metadiegetic information might include voiced thoughts (another kind of "voice-over") that the other characters cannot hear, images that clearly come from the mind of a character and which other characters cannot see, or sounds imagined by a character that other characters cannot hear. Metadiegetic devices are used to give the film spectator privileged information about a character. Although technically the narrator of a film story can be positioned inside the diegesis, in practice it would be very difficult to limit the details of the narration to the information that one person could know. Even when a story is told as the memory (in "flashback") of a character, the manner of telling almost always conforms to the conventions of the arranger.

Another set of conventions in film language has to do with space. While we are watching a film, we build up a three-dimensional mental model of the space in which the action is happening—the so-called diegetic space. Usually the spatial information is conveyed by the narrating camera which follows an identifiable style; for instance, David Bordwell's categories of film narration in *Narration in the Fiction Film* specifically differentiate the ways in which film space is constructed in each type.

When we speak of the film language of narrative films, we mean not only these conventions of storytelling, but also the conventions of shot to shot transition and the treatment of diegetic time and space, plot structure, and the like. Not all films follow the same conventions, however. Bordwell's typology distinguishes between the Hollywood film and the art cinema film. In discussing how any given film departs from convention, one has to be aware of the norm that defines the parameters of its type.

The literature of the postwar period has been characterized by a suspicion of language. From Samuel Beckett to Raymond Queneau and the French *nouveau roman*, there has been a tendency to make language itself the subject of literary works. This self-questioning of the artistic medium of expression finds its echo in film. In my first chapter I have attempted to show how Louis Malle, in his adaptation of Queneau's *Zazie dans le métro*, tries to do for film language what Queneau has done for literature: to purify it and liberate it from the strictures of convention. Malle's violation of norms is seen as a display of various types of frame-breaking.

In a second chapter I have chosen for discussion four films of the 1970s that echo the "poetics of silence" that Beckett practices as a defense against the false rationality of Western civilization. I argue that the ancient Greeks, who are credited with the creation of that rationality, realized from the beginning that it was a system that bore within itself the germ of its own destruction. I take the *Oedipus Rex* by Sophocles as evidence of the Greeks' own awareness of this tragic contradiction. The play expresses a lack of confidence in language as a method for finding the truth—a philosophical stance visually brought home in the films discussed. This discussion shows that the film medium is capable of dealing effectively with the challenge to language and expressiveness that is characteristic of some of the major literary works of our era.

CHAPTER

1

BREAKING THE FRAME
Zazie and Film Language

Louis Malle's 1960 version of Raymond Queneau's *Zazie dans le métro* (first published in 1959) offers a privileged opportunity for the investigation of cinematic language and its relation to literary language because it is not an adaptation in the usual sense. Instead of merely rendering the content of Queneau's novel, Malle proposed to break the conventions of cinematic narration in a manner analogous to Queneau's treatment of literary and linguistic conventions. Malle's aim (like Queneau's) was to criticize society and its cultural institutions: "The disintegration of traditional cinematic language was not only an exercise in style, but the most efficacious method of describing and parodying a world that was itself disintegrated and chaotic."[1]

In many ways Malle's film is an exponent of the coming together in France in the 1960s of the cinematic New Wave and what was to become the "new novel" (*nouvelle vague* and *nouveau roman*). The New Wave is a term given to a group of young filmmakers whose first feature films came out in 1959 or 1960. They owed their common spirit to the fact that many of them started off as film critics for the *Cahiers du cinéma* cofounded by André Bazin in 1951. Under Bazin's influence, such young critics/filmmakers as Jean-Luc Godard, François Truffaut, and Eric Rohmer developed the idea that films are authored rather than being the anonymous products of a studio. Their contribution to the historical understanding of film was the appreciation of the "authorial style" of American studio directors such as John Ford and Howard Hawkes and a deeper appreciation of the stylistic oeuvre of such European filmmakers as Roberto Rossellini and Vittorio de Sica (of the Italian neorealist school), Jean Renoir, Robert Bresson, and Jean Cocteau. Alexandre Astruc developed the concept of the *caméra stylo* (camera-pen) and argued that the technical apparatus of cinema can be used as an instrument of personal expression.

Somewhat paradoxically, the filmmakers most appreciated by the *Cahiers* critics were those who contributed to a greater appreciation of the real world. The *Cahiers* group advocated realism, but while many of its members started out by making documentaries, they quickly shifted to feature film production.

Still, most New Wave directors retain a *cinéma vérité* element in their fictional style while they simultaneously invent new film metaphors and pay homage in their films to the techniques of Hollywood films. Often, they play one style off against another. No matter how fictional their creations, their films are political in the sense that poetry and art are put in the service of understanding reality. *Zazie dans le métro* is a prime example of a film rich in political implications.

The New Wave emphasis on film as writing made it easy for filmmakers to collaborate with literary artists: Alain Resnais filmed *Hiroshima mon amour* with Marguerite Duras in 1959, and *Last Year at Marienbad* with Alain Robbe-Grillet in 1961. Both of these authors later became filmmakers in their own right. Although Queneau was of an older generation than the authors associated with the "new novel," his literary experiments have a lot in common with those of the new generation of Robbe-Grillet, Michel Butor, and Nathalie Sarraute.[2] *Zazie* is a brilliant example of fiction written in what Sarraute has called "the era of suspicion" ushered in by World War II and its aftermath. Sarraute writes that today's authors and readers distrust one another; the reader wants to know who is speaking, while the author feels constrained by the conventional typology that the reader inevitably brings to bear on any psychological narrative.[3] In his commentary on the *nouveau roman*, Stephen Heath has shown that the focus in these works was on various aspects of the literary: on literature as a type of writing, on the relationship between author and reader, and on the intertextual relations between literary texts: "In the space of the text in the practise of writing there is no longer a movement forward to the fixing of some final Sense or Truth, but on the contrary, an attention to a plurality, to a dialogue of texts, founding and founded in an intertextuality to be read in, precisely, a *practise* of writing."[4]

Queneau's *Zazie dans le métro* plays on the distrust of narrative authority by presenting a fourteen-year-old antagonist of the adult world. Dropped off at her uncle Gabriel's during her mother's romantic tryst in Paris, she refuses to be impressed by any outside authority. Her reaction to Napoleon's tomb sets the tone for her single-minded and madcap excursion through the city: "Napoléon mon cul . . . cet enflé, avec son chapeau à la con" ("Napoleon my arse . . . that old windbag with his silly bugger's hat," in Barbara Wright's remarkable English translation).

In the heroine's revolt, the narrator is her ally, creating phonetic word-puzzles (the first word of the novel, "Doukipudonktan," roughly translatable as "Howcantheystinkso"), and undermining the adults by making fun of their sense of their own importance. Queneau's radical attack on literary convention extends to language itself and suggests that society will not be sane until our very modes of expression have been shaken up and reformulated.

In a perceptive essay on Queneau's *Zazie*, Roland Barthes has pointed out that to attack literary language by writing a novel is, paradoxically, to restate the power of literary and linguistic expression. For Barthes, Zazie is the tool through which the cultural baggage of connotation and metalanguage is stripped of its suffocating power. He notes that the adults are unable to speak without using conventionalized expressions that come from the French cultural and literary past, whereas Zazie's discourse is either requesting or commanding, and has as its object an immediate effect on reality: "Zazie . . . is the refusal of lyrical (literary) language, the science of transitive language . . . she recalls to order."[5] Yet, if the character of Zazie allows Queneau to establish a point of reference for this "antilanguage," he knows that hers is a language that literature can never completely assume. As Barthes put it, Queneau's modernist stance consists in his uneasy alliance with literary forms: "He assumes the mask of literature, but at the same time he unmasks (points a finger at) it."[6]

To adopt yet another of Barthes's paradigms, Zazie is a writable text (texte scriptible) that can only be enjoyed by a reader who participates in the play of its significations.[7] Its mix of slang, spoken and literary French, neologisms, and phonetic puzzles challenges the reader's sensitivity to the nuances of the language.[8] Queneau's literary parodies and intertextual references provide yet another source of playful interaction between reader and text. In addition to the discourses enumerated by Barthes (Latin, medieval, epic, and Homeric), Zazie echoes Shakespeare and Sartre ("Being or nothingness, that is the question"), Racinian alexandrines ("I know this alexandrinarily: that they are almost dead since they are not here" ["les voilà presque morts puisqu'ils sont des absents]), and Lewis Carroll (portmanteau words such as "factidiversalité" for "faits divers," news items).

The polyphony of Queneau's texts pluralizes the linear progression of the readable text (texte lisible) and disperses its elements. Language explodes in the disruptive celebration of itself qua language, foregrounding its powers of expression and rejecting its traditional subordinate role in relation to plot and character. By inviting the reader's playful engagement in its network of significations, the novel presents itself as dialogical. Zazie dans le métro belongs to the type of modernist text that Julia Kristeva, in the wake of Mikhail Bakhtin, describes as "carnavalesque."In such texts, she argues, the linguistic code is transgressed by another system of signification derived from the logic of dreams—the unconscious.[9]

If I describe Queneau's language as playful and imbued with the logic of the unconscious, I do so with an ulterior motive, for these are characteristics of surrealism, a movement to which the young Queneau belonged in the 1920s. Founded in 1924 by André Breton, surrealism set out to transform everyday reality by the operations of the unconscious. Its adherents chose two ways of doing so: through works of art, literature, and film; and by their everyday living. In the arts, they attempted to create works that flowed directly from the unconscious, in the belief that the expression of untrammeled desire would necessarily be more free and truthful than works they could create according to the established canons of taste. Surrealist metaphors flowered forth in surprising juxtapositions hitherto unknown in literature, film, and painting. To the surrealists, the best part of life was childhood, before rational thought becomes oppressively dominant. They saw themselves as the revolutionary transformers of society, who would bring people back in touch with their true selves and liberate their enslaved creative energies.[10]

The surrealists did not limit themselves to experiments in art; they also attempted to live according to the dictates of the unconscious, looking, in real life, for chance encounters or strange coincidences that would prove to them that the unconscious with its lack of logic could provide a modus vivendi as well. In *Zazie*, it is obvious that surrealism left an indelible mark on Queneau. His heroine is a child who is refreshingly free of the constraints of the adult world and who uses language as a liberating force. Queneau's novel is full of the verbal inventiveness and disrespect of literary convention so characteristic of surrealism. But there is an additional dimension. The surrealists were dedicated to the idea that language could transform reality—their writings were exuberant expressions of their faith in the metamorphosis of consciousness that linguistic and mental liberation would bring. Appearing in the postwar period, Queneau's writings have a darker side. Like many other literary works of this period, his novels are ultimately self-effacing. They affirm the presence of language without staking out a claim either of continuity with the past or influence on the future. In this they are part of what Barthes has called "white writing" (*écriture blanche*)—a literature of silence. It is as though in the age of suspicion any serious literary work had to question its own voice.

In adapting *Zazie dans le métro*, Malle added to Queneau's vision his own critique of bourgeois complacency and life in the modern city. By violating cinematic conventions, Malle tries to communicate the insufficiency of our habitual representations of reality; and by proposing Zazie as the anti-heroine of Paris who questions everything the adults around her would have her believe he creates a focus for the spectator's identification that acts as a catalyst for the liberation of unconscious thoughts and feelings.

Zazie dans le métro was Malle's third feature film and remained one which he declared himself only partially satisfied.[11] Like many New Wave directors, Malle started out in documentary, working for a time as cameraman for Jacques Cousteau's *Le monde du silence* (1956). He has continued to make documentaries throughout his career; the best known, *L'Inde fantôme*, was produced in 1969. In fact, nearly all of Malle's fiction films preserve a documentary aspect. *Lacombe, Lucien* (1974) recreates the atmosphere of occupied France and the Resistance while *Atlantic City* (1980) captures that city's version of the American Dream. Malle's use of the French photographer Belocq as the protagonist in *Pretty Baby* (1977) gives him the opportunity to interweave with the story a photographic documentary of New Orleans and the milieu of prostitution in 1917. Many of Malle's "fictions" are in fact documentaries, just as his "documentaries" are fictions. He is conscious that, just as the act of filming implies subjectivity, any imaginary creation is colored by the surprise intrusion of the real: "If you put your camera in the street, the way you film is an interpretation. So it's your point of view, it's a mirror game—and it's terribly unconscious . . . I try to do it in fiction too now, as much as I can. I try to invent a world, I put my camera in front of it, and then try to shoot the way I'd shoot a documentary."[12]

Translating this statement into the terms presented above, we might say that Malle's fiction films disrupt the cinematic conventions of the narrative genre with those of documentary realism. *Zazie* is a film in which different expectations are constantly canceling one another out. Malle's major innovation in adapting Queneau's novel is the creation of a parodic film arranger who reveals himself at every moment as unreliable and subversive in relation to the basic rules of cinematic coherence. Like Queneau, whose models were Alfred Jarry, Lewis Carroll, and the comic strip, Malle is inspired by the cinematic precedents of Georges Méliès, Mack Sennett, Buster Keaton and the cartoon. In spirit, he is closest perhaps to Jean Vigo's *Zéro de conduite* (1933). Just as Queneau shifts registers, combining spoken French with the literary *passé simple*, neologisms and recherché vocabulary, Malle's style is a mixture of genres. As one critic put it: "This isn't a film, it's an anthology."[13] In this too, Malle rejoins the encyclopedism of Queneau's work, which often reads like a compendium of literary antecedents, scientific facts, and slang. Malle's painstaking dissection of cinematic language can be divided into three categories that derive from the preceding analysis: the disruption of the narrative frame, intertextual play between frames, and the irruption into the narrative of dream logic.

THE DISRUPTION OF THE NARRATIVE FRAME

Like Queneau, Malle foregrounds the medium of his art; the viewer is constantly reminded that he or she is at the cinema. Nowhere is this more apparent than in Malle's creation of a fantastical narrative space, time, and causality. The first scene shows Gabriel on a platform, surrounded by a band of "extras" who will reapppear in various guises throughout the film. As the camera pans slowly past them, it seems to be presenting them to us for review: a pickpocket, a man reading the journal *Diogène*, a fashionably dressed lady, a young woman resembling the famous cabaret singer Juliette Greco, a poor woman in a cap, and so on. The characters stand still, like figures in a wax museum, while the pickpocket moves past them in the direction of the camera's tracking shot, snatching objects from their hands and off their shoulders. Gabriel, having uttered the *Doukipudonktan* that opens Queneau's novel, wanders among these people while the camera follows him. He comes to stand again next to the man reading *Diogène*, who has had to cross behind the camera to rejoin Gabriel in this position, thus violating the principle of consistent diegetic space. This first incongruity of diegetic space prefigures similar effects throughout the film.

The train arrives, and Zazie's mother, Jeanne Lalochère, runs toward the open-armed Gabriel (Philippe Noiret) in a shot-counter-shot. At the last moment, the *Diogène* reader steps out from behind Gabriel and grabs Lalochère, bearing her off for the weekend while Gabriel is assaulted by Zazie. The rest of the film depicts Zazie's Parisian adventures for the next thirty-six hours before she is handed, sleepy and exhausted, to her mother who just barely makes the train back.

While in Paris, Zazie's main goal is to ride the métro (subway) which is on strike the day she arrives. The first morning, she escapes from Gabriel's house to go for a ride. Finding the strike still on, she pretends to cry (it is clear from the soundtrack that the tears are false). Adopted at once by a shady character named Pedro, she is taken to the flea market. Malle's descriptive shots again create an illogical diegetic space, as he cuts from rows of merchandise to rows of women under hairdryers. Later the women are seen next to the bistro where Gabriel lives, implying that the arranger has lifted the beauty shop from its real location in order to create a kind of cinematic joke through graphic matching. The emphasis on regular rows of objects recalls François Léger's cubist *Ballet mécanique* (1924) and René Clair's *Entr'acte* (1924); yet Malle's point is not abstraction but a violation of the norms of narrative: the script specifies that the purpose is "to give the impression of a mistake in the montage."[14]

Pedro buys Zazie a pair of blue jeans and then takes her to lunch in a bistro. At the end of her lunch, Zazie makes off with her *bloudjinnzes* (Queneau's spelling) with Pedro in hot pursuit. Zazie changes place at will during this chase scene which is reminiscent of Chaplin or Keaton. Similar disruptions of spatiality occur in Gabriel's apartment (Fig. 1), where she is shown seated alternately to the right and left of Gabriel, and in the final scene at the café, where her failure to appear in the place she supposedly occupies constitutes a violation of continuity.

Narrative time in Malle's film is equally illogical, even though the diegetic time of thirty-six hours is clearly delimited. When Zazie first makes her escape, she enters her room in pajamas and comes out a moment later fully dressed, despite the fact that no lapse of time has been implied in the diegesis.

Mismatching image and sound is another way of disturbing narrative coherence, and Malle makes the most of the opportunity by showing a man in the flea market who runs the bow of a violin against the arm of his suit while violin music is heard on the soundtrack. A shoe that Zazie picks up from a table plays a tune. Finally, writing is used to produce mismatches: a baby wears a sign "for sale" around its neck. It is as though Malle were offering the dissected elements of the film in separate parts so that the spectator can observe them dispassionately. The disjointed syllables that appear in the background of some shots in place of billboards graphically underline this dismemberment of language.

Malle even dissects bodies: the severed arms of mannequins adorn the bistro where Zazie has lunch. Even more disturbing are the shifts of identity: Pedro buys the blue jeans from his own double, Pedro-Surplus, as Malle manages to get the same actor in one frame playing two different roles. Later Pedro returns as the policeman Trouscaillon and finally as an Italian fascist soldier. Gabriel's wife is not only Albertine but Albert, to whom the departing Zazie throws a final "au revoir monsieur" at the end of the film.

1. Zazie at her uncle Gabriel's house with Marceline (Philippe Noiret, Catherine Demongeot, and Carla Marlier). (Louis Malle, *Zazie dans le métro*)

INTERTEXTUAL PLAY BETWEEN FRAMES

I have said that Malle, like Queneau, mixes registers in his film; for the most part he does this through the quotation of other films or film genres. The first shot is a traveling shot of the train tracks, giving the spectator a view from the train that brings Zazie to Paris. The image is accompanied by a whistled Western tune. The same shot, in reverse, ends the film. Through this repetition, Zazie emerges as the cool and pure heroine of a Western who comes into town, cleans up the place, and leaves.

Malle's own earlier films are ruthlessly parodied in *Zazie*. The policeman Trouscaillon sneaks into Gabriel's apartment to woo Albertine to the same Brahms sextet that accompanied the love scene between Jeanne Moreau and Jean-Marc Bory in the sentimental *Les Amants* (*The Lovers*, 1958) with the identical voice-over comment: "L'Amour peut naître d'un regard" (love can be born of a look). Zazie's long walk through Paris with the widow Mouaque who has fallen in love with Trouscaillon echoes a similar scene with Jeanne Moreau in Malle's *L'Ascenseur pour l'échafaud* (1958). But perhaps Malle's funniest parody is that of Alain Resnais's and Marguerite Duras's *Hiroshima mon amour* which had come out the previous year. While sitting in the bistro with Pedro, Zazie is describing the (imaginary) scene in which her mother killed her father with an axe. The parallel scene in the Duras/Resnais film is Riva's confession to Okada in which traveling shots of the Loire near Nevers are intercut with shots of the two characters in the bar at Hiroshima (see chapter 5). Malle makes a similar cut to a long traveling shot down a corridor at the end of which Zazie's father sits alone in chair. Zazie's words, heard in a voice-over, are similar to Riva's: "Papa he was all alone in the house, all alone he waited, he waited for nothing in particular, he waited just the same, and it was all alone he waited." (Riva: "I was waiting for you with a patience that knew no limits.") But where Riva, in a moment of great emotional intensity, is awakened from her memory of the past by Okada's slap, Zazie's father claps his hands in the air to kill a fly. At this point Zazie, like Riva, awakens from her reverie.

By referring to other films, Malle foregrounds this film as film. The metafilmic dimension of *Zazie* is enhanced by the actual appearance of cameramen, grips, and lighting crew in the final café scene where the fight between waiters, fascist soldiers, nightclub artists, and tourists results in the demolition of the café's decor. In other scenes one catches glimpses of "stars": the popular music singer Sacha Distel next to a billboard picture of himself and a woman strongly resembling Marilyn Monroe.

Queneau's parody of *Hamlet* profits from Malle's hilarious mise-en-scène on the Eiffel Tower in which Gabriel crawls over the balustrade and rides to the top on the roof of the elevator, declaiming all the while. Malle also parodies literary sources that Queneau does not mention. Albertine is described as "disparue" in a reference to Marcel Proust's *Albertine disparue*, one of the volumes of his *A la recherche du temps perdu*. One suspects that Malle changed Queneau's Marceline to Albertine solely for the Proustian overtones, in order to make a connection between that writer's homosexuality and the suggested homosexual relation between Gabriel and Albertine/Albert.

THE IRRUPTION OF DREAM LOGIC INTO THE NARRATIVE

Like Queneau, Malle uses humor as one of the main instruments of attack against convention. In *Jokes and Their Relation to the Unconscious*, Freud has shown how humor releases energy from the unconscious, giving rise to laughter. Malle's film gags and verbal jokes are related to the operations of the unconscious as Freud describes them: displacement, condensation, and figurative representation. His use of dream logic makes Malle as close as Queneau to the surrealists.

On a verbal level, Malle adopts many of Queneau's humorous effects from the novel. Displacement occurs in Gabriel's pithy résumé of the human condition, in which a series of similar sounds conceals the idea of futility and death by its seductive euphony: "Un rien l'amène. Un rien l'anime. Un rien l'em-mène."[15] The displacement of morphemes that mask the unmentionable (death) reveals that displacement is a form of censorship, as Freud has shown.[16] Malle finds cinematographic equivalents to Queneau's literary expression in his ma-nipulation of the soundtrack. When Zazie first meets Turandot, the owner of the bistro in which Gabriel occupies a second-floor apartment, she lets out a stream of insult that is played backwards on the soundtrack so it cannot be understood. A similar effect is achieved by masking words with the sound of a truck in the scene where Zazie escapes Turandot's pursuit by suggesting to a crowd of people that he has made indecent overtures to her. We never get to hear the monstrosity that is passed around in a whisper by the shocked and fascinated adults.

On the visual plane, Malle's portrayal of Pedro/Trouscaillon/Mussolini is a form of displacement. On reflection, the spectator realizes that Pedro's previous association with a mugging (in his first scene with Zazie), interrogation (his abuse of the shoemaker Gridoux and of Gabriel), authoritarianism (his behavior in the traffic jam), and despotism (his attempted seduction of Albertine in Gabriel's dressing room with its picture of Napoleon on the wall) have been clues to his concealed identity of a fascist murderer throughout the film. The refusal of people to recognize the many faces of fascism for what they are is a theme Malle would take up again in *Lacombe, Lucien*.

Verbal condensation occurs in the film when Malle mixes registers of speech—a favorite technique of Queneau's. Here the humor arises not from the spec-tator's recognition of a defiance of censorship (as in displacement) but in the pleasure derived from recognizing the economical compression of psychic en-ergy. Gabriel's monologue on the Eiffel Tower offers one of the best examples: "Forceps bore them, a hearse carried them away, and the Tower rusts and the Panthéon cracks more rapidly than the bones of the dead who are too much with us dissolve in the humus of the town impregnated with cares."[17] The inflated language and histrionic declamation are partially negated by the banal "the Tower rusts."

Malle's visual condensations have the power of surrealist metaphor. In the scene at the Eiffel Tower, Gabriel stands by a sea captain who is looking out into the void with his telescope. Suddenly, a wave breaks against the railing, transforming the Eiffel Tower platform into the deck of a ship (Fig. 2). In another scene, a busload of tourists becomes, in succession, an airplane (a stewardess begins handing out lunchtrays) and a sitting at the United Nations (the tour-guide's comments sputter forth in several different languages through the tour-ists' headphones).

The dream logic of this film also includes the figurative representation of concepts not expressed in words but translated into visual images. This is especially true of the use of color: Gabriel's apartment in the Pigalle section of Paris changes color with the flashing neon lights behind the window, giving the impression that the inhabitants are fish in an aquarium. The tacit comparison of people to animals is continued in the parrot who spouts the famous line from

2. A wave washes up to the Eiffel Tower. (Louis Malle, *Zazie dans le métro*)

the novel: "Tu causes, tu causes, c'est tout ce que tu sais faire" (talk, talk, that's all you can do), and who, in Malle's version, plays telephone operator. To the person who complains about the parrot, Turandot replies: "You should see a psittaco-analyst." This "beastification" of humans is an idea dear to Queneau, whose long poem *Petite cosmogonie portative* (1969) reveals a fascination for animals other than human, while the aquarium theme is important in *Gueule de Pierre* (1934), the first part of Queneau's trilogy *Saint Glinglin*.

In many ways, the disruption of narrative, the use of intertextuality, and the irruption of dream logic can all be seen as a shifting between the subframes of the text. Malle's compression of time and space, in which distant places become contiguous by "errors of montage" is a form of dream logic. It is also intertextual: when Zazie walks right off the street into Gabriel's bedroom in a single traveling shot, the effect reminds us of Buñuel's incongruous narrative space in *Un Chien andalou* (1928). The dreamlike wish-fulfillment of Zazie as she throws her shoes up in the air to see them land on her feet all buckled up is a disruption of narrative causality that also has an intertextual dimension: the scene in Vigo's *Zéro de conduite* where the childlike imagination of the arranger has the power to make cartoon drawings move of their own accord while rubber balls stay up in the air without any visible means of support. The film spectator is clearly a part of whatever play of signification is initiated by the text: by using dream logic to break up the narrative, by transmitting information through an unreliable arranger and creating characters who either change their identity or do not seem firmly anchored in narrative space, Malle has clearly succeeded in his goal of avoiding the "narcotic effect of cinema" where the spectator is the recipient of a spectacle designed to produce passive gratification.[18]

It remains to be considered whether Malle has accomplished his goal of providing a cinematic equivalent to Queneau's disintegration of literary language. To this end I shall juxtapose two contrary views that appeared in the *Cahiers du Cinéma* just after the release of the film.

The negative review by André Labarthe takes the position that Malle's disintegration of cinematic language becomes a cinematic representation of the disintegration of reality—a representation that never calls into question the problem of film language. Moreover, Labarthe claims that this failure stems from the very nature of the film medium: "Since the cinema is the art of the real *par excellence*, any critique of its language must necessarily become an interrogation of the real."[19] It is difficult to admit this position on philosophical grounds. Labarthe seems to suggest that film spectators cannot tell the difference between the play on intertextual and narrative frames that I have described above and challenges to the conceptual frames that we use in getting about in the real world.

A different position is taken by Mars in his three-part series, "L'autopsie du gag." Mars stresses how Malle uses the film gag to interrupt the narrative so that an alert spectator is constantly made aware of the play of cinematic language at the expense of diegetic linearity:

> Zazie is not . . . a retrospective of the gag . . . but an attempt at a new cadence, a new style whose principal advantage is to show that a gag does not need to be integrated into an action, that it can suffice as an action in itself. Pushed to the limits of the absurd, this would mean that one hundred and eighty thirty-second gags, aligned one after the other without any concern for coherence, would not constitute a coherent film of an hour and a half, but a festival of one hundred and eighty different films, lasting thirty seconds each.[20]

Malle's new "cadence" is in effect the constant shifting between frames that I have described above. Returning once again to Barthes, it is possible to say just as forcibly of Malle's *Zazie* that it is the work of obsessional *découpage*.[21] In the film version, however, it is not the character Zazie who wipes the slate clean with her disruptive language, but the arranger who undermines the narrative logic with the logic of dreams and intertextual references. Like Queneau, Malle knows there is no safe position outside language—language is attacked from within, by the interplay of frames. As Metz has said, "A text is nothing but a series of divergences."[22]

Malle's film has, of course, the support of Queneau's verbal inventiveness. His success can be measured by the way he has integrated the other four channels of cinematic signification (image, sound, music, and writing) into his "translation." Like the métro of Zazie's desire, language is "on strike" in Malle's film—as in Queneau's novel.

CHAPTER
2

FILM WRITING AND
THE POETICS OF SILENCE

Louis Malle's consciousness of the disjunction between language and reality expressed itself in an effervescent cinematic discourse, a heroic attempt to cover over the gap with the brash antics of his heroine Zazie and with a film style that celebrated diversity, surprise effects, and comic references to the history of cinema. Other filmmakers have had quite a different reaction to self-consciousness; if Malle attempts to save himself (and his art) through comedy, these filmmakers seem more allied with a tragic vision.

In this chapter I will be discussing a group of films that seem related as though by metaphor. Although each is by a recognized film author, they enact, in turn, a poetics of silence—the cinematic equivalent of Barthes's "white writing." Among these I would count *Last Tango in Paris* (*Le Dernier tango à Paris*, Bernardo Bertolucci, 1972), *Apocalypse Now* (Francis Ford Coppola, 1979), *Kings of the Road* (*Im Lauf der Zeit*, Wim Wenders, 1976), and *Quintet* (Robert Altman, 1979). What these films have in common is a moment in which the characters in them reach the farthest outpost of civilization, beyond which meaning ceases. Each one seems to exist, as Stanley Cavell puts it, "in a condition of philosophy."[1]

In their orientation toward the tragic and in their search for the meaning of Western civilization, these works are part of the tradition that began with Sophocles' dramatization of the myth of Oedipus. In the Oedipus plays, I shall argue, Sophocles put into dramatic form the way language was born out of the Greek city. If today that language seems increasingly called into doubt, this was an outcome already foretold by the Greek dramatist. The universally felt anxiety about the status of any discourse, whether it takes the form of a literary work or a film, was foreseen by Sophocles. His plays reflect the realization that manmade rationality would only offer a temporary shelter against the forces that wait on the destruction of civilization.

Yet, despite their pessimism, each of these works ends on a note of hope. This hope takes various forms: a hope for radical change (Wenders), for salvation through confrontation with the unknown (Altman) or from some clue to be found in memory, through a reexamination of the past (Bertolucci, Coppola). In each of the films, the filmmaker has tried to forge a new reality, while being restricted to the language of cinema. In that sense, each has contributed to a project first outlined by the French critic André Bazin: that of allowing the screen to function as a window, letting reality transpire through it, while at the same time ensuring that that filmed reality should be a *visioned* reality, a heightened and intensified experience of the real.

Bazin's injunctions influenced a whole generation of filmmakers from the French New Wave onward. The filmmaking practice he advocated is political in the broadest sense of the term. To write with the intention of fusing language and reality is to write with a sense of the civic community, of the *polis*. In Bazin, realism becomes the battlecry, the political engagement which serves to define the great cinematic author. Only those directors who have furthered the cause of realism in cinema are awarded the distinction of being called "authors" in Bazin's system. His famous phrase *la politique des auteurs* comes to have two meanings: the impetus for seeking out and consecrating individual directors is a political one in that the approximation of cinema to the real will be furthered by it; at the same time, Bazin implies that the realist tendencies of those very authors stemmed from a political commitment on their part.[2]

The four films I will be discussing stand on a kind of threshold. Although each is the creation of an expressive film author, each in turn questions the possibility of saying anything at all, either because the reality they seek to portray seems beyond any verbal or cinematic language, or because their very subject is itself the limitations of cinematic expression. Although these themes run throughout each work, there is a moment in which they reach a crisis.

In *Apocalypse Now* that crisis comes when Captain Willard, proceeding up the river to Kurtz's hideout, comes upon a battle taking place over the water at Do Lung Bridge (Fig. 3). A string of lights is the only apparently significant demarcation between the two sides of the battle, but none of the soldiers questioned knows who is in charge or where the enemy line begins. I take this to be a metaphor for the limits of meaning per se, when all difference and hierarchy is effaced. Beyond this line, Willard says, is only Kurtz, a man gone insane whom the natives worship as a god.

A similar moment occurs in *Im Lauf der Zeit*. The Wenders film is the recounting of several months of companionship between two men (Fig. 4). In the opening shots of the film, Robert drives his VW beetle straight into a lake and sinks it. At the edge of the lake Bruno stands beside his truck shaving. Intrigued by the action of Robert, he offers him a ride. This, in turn, gives Robert the opportunity to explain the details of the marital breakup which have upset him. Bruno makes his living by fixing the projectors in village movie theaters, a profession that allows Wenders to make comments on the movie industry: the film begins with a sort of prologue, an interview between Bruno and a film theater owner, a former Nazi, whose theater was shut down after the war. It closes with another interview at the *Weisse Wand* (white screen) film theater whose owner refuses to show the films that are sent to her by

3. The point where meaning ceases: the battle at Do Lung Bridge. (Francis Ford Coppola, *Apocalypse Now*)

distributors, films, she says, "in which people lose all sense of themselves and of the world." Nevertheless, she keeps her theater in working order in case good films begin to be made again. Bruno decides, upon hearing this, to quit his job. As he drives away his windshield reflects the "WW" of the *Weisse Wand* (white screen) theatre, which are also the initials of Wim Wenders.

Quintet posits an end-of-the-world scenario in which the last remaining outpost of human habitation is frozen in an ice age or nuclear winter. In the city survivors have taken up a deadly game by which the gamemaster establishes a roster of murders to be performed (Fig. 5). According to the rules of the game, you cannot kill out of turn, but you may avert your own death by killing your assigned murderer just before s/he kills you. The "hero" who returns to the city after a long absence accidentally assumes the place of one of the "players" and manages to win the game in progress by skillful self-defense. But rather than stay on to practice his skill as player, he sets off alone across the ice.

Last Tango in Paris takes place mainly in a practically empty apartment on the outskirts of the city where two people who were out apartment hunting become lovers. The character played by Marlon Brando refuses to know the girl's name (I use the word "girl" advisedly, since there is a continual play on her status as child-woman—only at the end does Tom, her fiancé, say that they

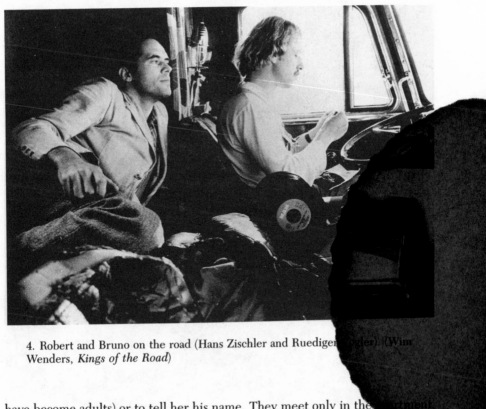

4. Robert and Bruno on the road (Hans Zischler and Ruediger ⬛⬛⬛⬛). (Wim Wenders, *Kings of the Road*)

have become adults) or to tell her his name. They meet only in the ⬛⬛⬛⬛ which he attempts to cut off from history and from the past. As in *Im⬛⬛⬛⬛ Zeit*, a telephone left connected serves to accentuate their lack of com⬛⬛⬛ cation, as they listen to each other's silence at opposite ends of the apartme⬛⬛ His own wife, the proprietress of a seedy hotel, has just killed herself by slitting her wrists with a razor. Throughout the film, the Brando character seems in a state of aphasia and shock, until the girl he is pursuing finally shoots him.

It seems to me that each of these films enacts the moment when words fail and when meaning dissolves with the disappearance of the differences between words and things that enable meaning to exist. They enact the failure of language and presage new possibilities of representation, of subjectivity, without actually finding a solution. They are philosophical in that they bring to the foreground an element of Western culture that philosopher Stanley Cavell has problematized in his writings. In particular, I believe that each of these works relates to the issues that Cavell raises in his discussion of Samuel Beckett's *Endgame*, for each in turn enacts a moment in which the there is something like a final throw of the dice.

That element is language, or what since the time of the Greeks has been called *logos*. I have said that I find these films to be united by a common metaphor, the metaphor of the birth of language as the ordering force of the

5. Quintet players (Paul Newman, Bibi Anderson, and Nina van Pallandt).
(Robert Altman, *Quintet*)

world. Its principal myth, I believe, is that of Oedipus as dramatized in the
trilogy of Sophocles: the *Oedipus Rex*, the *Antigone*, and the *Oedipus at Colonus*. These plays, I would argue, can be understood as the representation of
a conflict between language and the city, a conflict that led to the new practice
of an urban language that became the linchpin of our civilization and which
now finds itself under attack in philosophy, in psychoanalysis, in linguistics,
and in works of art such as the four films I have cited above.

Historically, one can speak of the dramatization, in the work of Sophocles, of the formation of the new human order—the political entity of Athens that ushered in a new kind of language. It was to celebrate that order that these plays were initially performed, as part of a religious festival. Not surprisingly, they deal with the very principles that made Greek civilization, from which our own derived, different from any other.

As Jean-Pierre Vernant explains in *Les Origines de la pensée grècque* (*The Origins of Greek Thought*), the growth of the city entailed several radical changes. First of all, the reception hall of the Homeric kings was replaced by the agora of the city—the marketplace where citizens could meet on a daily basis to discuss political issues. Then, writing inevitably led to the concept of historicity and to the consciousness of living in historical time. Finally, with the growth of a professional class, natural science replaced the idea of a mythic origin of humankind with a new view of them as a constituent part of the natural world.[3]

In the agora, speech became the agent of change—through speech, men attempted to alter concrete political facts. To this reality corresponded a new language. Sophocles' task in the three works centering around the Oedipus myth will be to liberate this new language from the mythical practices that preceded it and to establish the reputation of Athens as the privileged place where this language is spoken and flourishes.

There are three levels of language mentioned in the *Oedipus Rex*, and they are set in dialectical opposition to one another.[4] *Logos* is the rational speech that Oedipus champions over *chresmos*, the oracle, and *ainigma*, the riddle. Oedipus believes in, and identifies with, his own language. To Tiresias he boasts: "I came, know-nothing Oedipus, directed by my own thought rather than gaining my knowledge from the birds." His beginnings in Thebes seem to justify this optimism, for he has vanquished the Sphinx with his words and thought. Hegel, in *The Philosophy of History*, equated the Sphinx with the irrational. She comes from Egypt, from pre-Greek times:

> In the Egyptian [Goddess] Neith, Truth is still a problem. The Greek Apollo is its solution; his utterance is: "*Man, know thyself*" . . . Wonderfully, then, must the Greek legend surprise us, which relates that the Sphinx—the great Egyptian symbol—appeared in Thebes, uttering the words: *What is that which in the morning goes on four legs, at midday on two, and in the evening on three.* Oedipus, giving the solution, *Man*, precipitated the Sphinx from the rock.[5]

In the fourth century gloss on the play by Aristophanes the grammarian, the Sphinx herself practically gives away the answer to her riddle. She says: "There is a two-footed creature on the earth which is also a four-foot, *and has a voice*, and a three-foot" (esti dipoun epi ges kai tetrapon, *hou mia fone*, kai tripon). Taking the cue, Oedipus answers straight off: "Hear, whether you want or not, my *voice*"—thus making the text of the enigma into the instrument of its own solution.[6]

But all too soon Oedipus, whose strength relies upon language, finds that his own logos reverts to a riddle. For example he says that he may after all (despite all evidence) be innocent of Laios's murder because the witness mentioned several assailants and "one man can't be the same as many, of course." This turns into a riddle and an irony because the sophistry meant to ward off punishment makes him look for exactly the details (the shepherd's story) which will show him to be "the same as" brother and father to his children. In this way he falls victim to his own language, as the Sphinx did. Oedipus defends himself against the irony of Tiresias and against Creon, the second-in-command, because he foresees that his defeat will entail the defeat of the new city he represents: "You intend to betray me and let the city die." The new city, the new urban language, will in the end not be founded at Thebes, from which Oedipus is banished.

It will, in fact, be founded at Athens. In the *Oedipus at Colonus*, Oedipus arrives at the sacred grove at Colonus outside Athens. When the Chorus first discovers him, they are horrified because his curse defiles their sacred place. But Oedipus explains that the special nature of his sin can be turned to the profit of the city that honors him. The Chorus argues Oedipus's case before Theseus, the ruler of Athens, and wins. At the end Oedipus is carried off by the Gods somehow. His instructions are that no one should know the place of his death except Theseus; as long as the secret is kept Athens will be secure. From now on, the city will be justified and protected by a sacred element exterior to it, element that has to do with the violent disruption of the old order. Logos triumphs and is installed at Athens.

By leaving Oedipus outside the city Sophocles implicitly sets up the possibility of the continuance of a dialectic between the forces (the Gods) that doomed and saved him; the situation suggests the same sort of insta-bility as the hero's limp, which one feels obliged to take into account in any interpretation of the myth. With uncanny prescience Sophocles intimates that urban man and the language he wields stand on somewhat shaky legs. If the Greek philosophers, as Foucault and Derrida have argued, opted for a *logos* to which there was no alternative,[7] I understand Sophocles to predict a return of those repressed elements of the dialectic that the establishment of logos had negated.

The disequilibrium that always threatens this delicate balance is dramatized in the last play of the trilogy, the *Antigone*. Here the heroine insists on burying the corpse of her insurgent brother against the explicit orders of Creon. Successful politics, Sophocles shows, can only come about through shared language. Statesmanship is equated with the skilled practice of language, in the famous hymn to the accomplishments of man who may have "speech and wind-quick thought and city-strengthening anger" (353). The failure of Creon and Antigone to come to terms is a failure of language. Haemon, the king's son, argues with Creon that the voice of the city speaks against him; Creon responds that he is the sole ruler ("whoever the city has established, he should be listened to.") Haemon's answer, "anyone who thinks he's the only one with a mind or a tongue or a soul, when unfolded proves empty" (707), neatly summarizes the Athenian notion of democratic political rule, an ideal not yet achieved in Thebes. Sophocles shows that, in the absence of a shared language, humankind is doomed to incomprehension and suffering.

In our own century, from the surrealists to Ionesco, from the plays of Jean Anouilh to the novels of Alain Robbe-Grillet, literature has proclaimed that the connection between language and reality has been lost. Orthodox surrealists such as André Breton pursued the irrational Freudian rather than the rational Hegelian Oedipus: gain access to your unconscious, they said, and creative forces will be liberated that will enable you to transcend the rationalist prison that encloses you. The languages of art, transformed by automatic modes of composition, will give back to artists the mirror of their true, unconscious selves. The surrealists share with the theater of the absurd a lack of concern for representation, and the use of language as a discovery mechanism that will transcend conventional categories. Yet the surrealists still hoped to forge a new relation between the self and the world, an ambition that the theater of the absurd abandoned to become pure language play, a document of our enslavement to words. The lost relation between language and reality is vividly illustrated by the modern version of *Antigone* by Anouilh, in which Creon says: "Nothing is true except that which is left unsaid."[8] His Antigone and his Creon are left with the sterile accomplishment of their scripted roles in a world where meaning has fled.[9]

Alain Robbe-Grillet brings the dissolution of the relation between language and reality one step nearer in *Les Gommes* (*The Erasers*), a novel in which the pretense of representation is continually erased, as the title suggests.[10] What makes this novel interesting for the present discussion is that the author includes over a hundred references, both obvious and veiled, to the Oedipus. But with the unraveling of the plot, the reader comes to realize that the multiple allusions to Oedipus were mere ploys. The reader of Robbe-Grillet's novels finds that the narrative is about the reading. In this work, the Sphinx has come back to haunt us, the plague has returned to attack language itself. Literature sets itself in motion to search for the cause but finds that the core of the disease lies within literature. When Claudio Guillén writes: "Civitas verbi: artistic wholes and literary systems are, like great cities, complex environments and areas of integration,"[12] he is talking about the sort of art work that it is no longer possible to write.

Thus the "age of suspicion" described by Nathalie Sarraute[13] strikes film as well. In my discussion of the four films I have mentioned, I take as my point of departure Stanley Cavell's remarks on Beckett's *Endgame*, in particular his statement that the main character of that play, Hamm (or "homme," man—since, as Cavell notes, *ha'am* is Hebrew for "the people) "presents a new image of what the mind, in one characteristic philosophical mood, has always felt like—crazed and paralyzed." *Endgame* shows us where logic got us.[14]

Robert Altman's *Quintet* links human fate to the fate of the city. Everything

6. Essex and his wife (Brigitte Fossey) arrive in the city. (Robert Altman, *Quintet*)

in the city is based on the number five: there are five sectors, twenty-five levels, and one can find any person by knowing just five numbers and a color code (Fig. 6). Filmed in Montreal's "Family of Man" exhibit from the World's Fair (and in the experimental apartment dwelling "habitat"), the ice-covered environment is a perfect representation of the end of technology. The game of quintet itself, which has become the sole focus of interest and purpose for these dying vestiges of humanity—amid which a train buried in snow literally signifies "the end of the line"—is based on five sectors, in the middle of which there is a "killing circle" surrounded by an area called "limbo" which is marked off into fields. The five players roll dice, trying to get a combination of five, and move around the board. The "killing order" is determined by the sixth player—the "sixth man," similar to the "dummy" in bridge, who plays the "survivor." In the tournaments played at the Casino, the game has become literal: the "players" are actually expected to kill each other off, and the five sectors of the city become the board on which the "game" is played.

Altman's hero Essex is a man who returns to the city after a long absence, in the company of his young wife (she is said to be "the youngest person alive," and she is pregnant). What Essex doesn't know is that the brother he visits has just been selected for a tournament, and within a few moments of the hero's arrival, his wife is killed in a deadly attack on the brother's family. Essex is the only survivor. His search to avenge his wife's death brings him ever closer to the truth, as he comes to realize the true meaning of the game. Altman is careful to limit the spectator's knowledge, so that he or she barely knows more than Essex knows. To follow the plot of the film thereby becomes a cognitive exercise in which the spectator identifies with Essex's progressive enlightenment and discovery.

I have said that none of the films I will discuss end on a note of pessimism; having found out the truth and killed all the other players, Essex starts out across the ice toward the unknown. This unknown is represented metaphorically as a goose which is seen at the beginning of the film, flying north to what seems like certain death. Yet the unknown also offers the possibility of hope, a chance to solve the dilemma of life. It is toward this hope that Essex sets off northward, stalking the goose through the frozen world. *Quintet* can be said to be part of the same philosophical project as *Endgame*: "Solitude, emptiness, nothingness, meaninglessness, silence—these are not the givens of Beckett's characters but their goal, their new heroic undertaking."

Bertolucci's *Last Tango in Paris* recasts another theme of Beckett's—that of "life outside the shelter (of authority, family, place, sanity)."[16] Paul refuses to know even the name of the young woman he meets in the bare apartment; they invent their lives from ground zero. "There's nobody here anymore," he tells an anonymous caller over the phone, "*il n'y a plus personne.*" Paul's shock at his wife's suicide stems from his realization that he never knew her. Women are always pretending either that they know who you are or that you don't know who they are, he complains to Jeanne. He wants to eliminate all games, to take the chance of loving someone he doesn't know.

In the end, Paul follows Jeanne to her mother's apartment after their "last tango" in a dance hall (Fig. 7). Panicking at the thought that she won't be able to get rid of him, she shoots him. At the end, she tonelessly recites what she will tell the police ("I don't know who it is, I don't know his name"). Yet this is only one side of the equation. At the other side is Jeanne's relation with Tom, the young man who wants to marry her and who is making a film about her (Fig. 8). The two films, Tom's and Bertolucci's, sometimes become one, as in the moment when Tom drops the mike and the enframing film—*Last Tango*—also loses its sound. I find it significant, and perhaps even hopeful, that Tom's attempt to forge a link to the future through memory of the past is posed against Paul's indifference to and denial of the past. While making his film, Tom encourages Jeanne to relive her childhood and sends her back through time in a replay of Cocteau's *Orphée*. Later, he throws a life preserver over Jeanne which is marked with the name of the boat in Jean Vigo's film about a young marriage, *L'Atalante*. Bertolucci suggests that memory may be the way out of the dilemmas of the past, although this solution is presented ambiguously through the somewhat comic presentation of Tom and because the life preserver, when thrown into the water, sinks.

The death of Paul, the suicide of Rosa become the equivalents of the mythic sacrifice that precedes the birth of language. To put it another way, Rosa and

7. The last tango (Maria Schneider and Marlon Brando). (Bernardo Bertolucci, *Last Tango in Paris*)

8. Tom (Jean-Pierre Léaud) filming a scene. (Bernardo Bertolucci, *Last Tango in Paris*)

Paul are the tragic heroes, Tom and Jeanne the common folk—the chorus—that can live because the ritual sacrifice has been made. "You're all alone," Paul says to Jeanne, "until you look up the ass of death, until you find a womb of fear." Sacrificing him is the compromise that Jeanne makes with normality; she puts aside the attraction she feels for Paul in order to settle comfortably with the clichés of what she herself calls "a pop culture marriage" based on the false promises of advertising.

Although Jeanne is attracted to Paul, Bertolucci shows that her fascination ultimately threatens to imprison her. Paul's repeated denials of the past are attempts to establish freedom, yet the apartment becomes like a cage for Jeanne (Bertolucci underscores this theme in scenes where they behave like wild animals). The weight of Paul's past continually surfaces, especially when he turns toward more violent forms of sexual expression. The viewer realizes, though Jeanne does not, that much of Paul's behavior is a reaction to the crisis brought about by his wife's suicide and to the marginal existence settled even before that as the "kept husband" (living side by side with the kept lover) in a hotel that serves a clientele of prostitutes and drug dealers.

Bertolucci metaphorically represents a world emptying itself of sense through small but noticeable details of the mise-en-scène. Throughout most of the film, a large object looms in the back of the apartment, covered by a white sheet. This object offers the promise of discovery. Although Paul looks under the sheet when he first comes to the apartment, the spectator's knowledge is restricted to the point of view of Jeanne, who does not look. Only when Jeanne discovers that Paul has moved all of his furniture out does she pull down the sheet in an act of frustration. But the objects under the sheet (a headboard and some other furniture) are disappointing, to her as well as to the film viewer.

The director also uses the sound and movement of aboveground means to accentuate the impersonality of Paul's and Jeanne's relationship. Between the credit sequence and the film's first shot, we hear the train; the camera then zooms down from a high angle on Paul to show him holding his ears to escape the sound of the train. Jeanne passes him on the sidewalk bordered by the pylons that hold up the train tracks. After he and Jeanne first make love in the apartment, a shot slowly pans from her leaving on street level, up to his separate departure on a bridge, and continuing upward, shows the departure of a train. After a violent lovemaking scene later in the film, Bertolucci cuts to two trains veering off in different directions. When Jeanne leaves the apartment after discovering the departure of Paul, he is waiting for her again under the pylons; visually Bertolucci makes it clear that the intense confrontation between these two individuals is drawing to a close. Significantly, their meeting from the beginning is a chance encounter, made possible by the social fabric of the city in which they live.

Although Jeanne ends up the survivor, Bertolucci hints that Paul is actually the stronger figure, for he has faced life's absurdity. At the same time Jeanne's ability to respond to Paul shows that she will never really believe in the superficial happiness that her pending marriage promises her.

Cavell writes that what Hamm sees is that "salvation lies in the ending of endgames, the final renunciation of all final solutions."[17] This is what I take to be the import of Francis Ford Coppola's *Apocalypse Now*, a film in which more is at stake than in the first two because it dares to take up the subject of the United States' war in Vietnam. The voice-over narration presents the first-person story of a certain Captain Willard sent upriver into Cambodia to assassinate a former war hero now gone mad, who is being worshipped among the stone monuments of Cambodia as a god. In order to tell this story, Coppola __s deep into myth; Kurtz has based his pretense of godhood on readings from the Bible, *The Golden Bough, From Ritual to Romance*, and T. S. Eliot. Once he finds him, Willard kills him in a ritual sacrifice which is intercut with the sacrifice of a water buffalo performed simultaneously by the natives. Coppola assimilates the story of Willard's ritual murder with that of the totem killing of the father as described in Freud's *Totem and Taboo*: having killed Kurtz, Willard is adored as the new god, father of the tribe. But Willard returns to civilization, leaving behind him the knowledge that Kurtz, at least, has come face to face with the madness that erupted within our own civilization. As in *Quintet*, there are dead bodies everywhere in Kurtz's camp. This "god" has chosen a language beyond words to express himself, because "it is impossible through words to describe what is necessary to those who do not know what horror means . . . horror and moral terror are your friends; if they are not, then they are enemies to be feared."

The uncertainty of words, of conventional supports is one that Coppola imposes on us in the bridge scene I have mentioned, and which draws us into the state of cognitive uncertainty that Willard experiences. As Miriam Hansen has written, we as spectators "may feel encircled and disembodied ourselves, temporarily dislocated from the safe ground in front of the screen."[18] That this uncertainty is a metacommentary on the authority of the cinema spectacle itself from an earlier attack scene in which Coppola himself plays the role of a television newsman filming the attack: "Don't look at the camera," he shouts to the bewildered soldiers, "just go by like you're fighting." Like Bertolucci, Coppola calls upon the cultural memory of his audience, producing quotations of Herzog's *Aguirre, the Wrath of God* (the boat which goes in circles after its captain has been killed), *8 1/2* (self-referential film), *Dr. Strangelove*, and many literary references.[19] Yet the effect is different; in this film the past is not set up to save us. Coppola's Kurtz recites the Eliot poem that takes a line from Conrad's original Kurtz, in *Heart of Darkness*, as an epigraph. The voice is paralyzed, in Eliot's "The Hollow Men" as in the aporia that was our involvement in Vietnam: a failure of *logos*, of language: "Our dried voices, when we whisper together, are quiet and meaningless . . . Shape without form, shade without colour, paralysed force, gesture without motion."

Coming from the killing of Kurtz, ritually daubed in variegated hues of mud, Willard holds the writings of his victim like Moses (Charlton Heston) holding the stone tablets in the 1956 Cecil B. DeMille film *The Ten Commandments*. His face is half darkened, as Kurtz's was. Like Beckett's Hamm, like Oedipus, Willard must take the place of the god. This is no facile exploration of a man gone over to the "dark side," as the officers who brief Willard suggest; it is a reenactment of the brutal forces that attend the birth of civilization and that, perhaps, also wait on its destruction. Coppola shows that Vietnam was an "endgame," played for real stakes. It was a game in which the myths that held our society together came apart, "a problem," as Cavell says of Beckett, "developing in our relation to our own words."[20] Words like freedom or democracy? Willard will bear Kurtz's knowledge back with him and become the author of his confession, the "caretaker of his memory." Only for this hope of a new beginning has Kurtz allowed him to live.

Nowhere better than in *Im Lauf der Zeit*, perhaps, do we come close to the actual mise-en-scène of Beckett's *Endgame*. The two friends have decided to spend the night on the tightly guarded border between East and West Germany, in an abandoned United States Army bunker. The walls are covered with scrawled messages that serve to accentuate the placelessness of American soldiers on German soil: their lack of belonging, of connection to any space to which they could meaningfully relate. Bruno actually manages to reconnect the telephone wires in order to call his estranged wife. But he gives up on the project: contact with the outside world appears impossible from this place, which seems to exist outside time and space. The two men in the bunker wait out the dawn. They can go no further—they have come to the edge of their world and ours, the barbed wire fence separating the two Germanys. In this lonely spot Robert explains to Bruno that he is a language specialist, that he treats children whose mental disturbances show up in their writing, in the stories they are able to tell about the letters they form. The letter "I" is a woman, Bruno suggests, "mean as she can be." And he poses himself a riddle: what he wants is to be both with a woman and alone. Both one and two, we hear the Sphinx say in the background, what is the animal . . . ?

In the morning Robert leaves the bunker and goes to the bus stop where he observes a young boy writing. He arranges to trade all his possessions for the boy's notebook. On the door of the bunker he has left this message for Bruno: "Everything must change," *alles muss anders werden.*

What is striking about each of these films is the fact that, while they attest to the seeming impossibility of reconciling life and language, they end on a note of hope; each in its own way announces a new beginning. This too is consistent with the spirit of Beckett's play as Cavell understands it: "The end of the game will be to show that the game has no winner . . . that games, plays, stories, morals, art—all the farcing of coherent civilizations—come to nothing, are nothing. To accomplish this will seem—will be—the end of the world, of *our* world. The motive, however, is not death, but life, or anyway human existence at last."[21]

PART TWO

REPRESENTATION

As a latecomer to the languages of art, film language is in many ways the most complex. It is visual as dance and painting are; it can tell stories as the novel can; like the theater it often involves actors. At the same time most feature films are composed of photographs of real objects (film theorists call this "pro-filmic reality") and hence become in some sense documents of the time in which they were made. The film theorist Christian Metz has argued that a complete theory of cinema should include sociology, the history of culture, and a knowledge of aesthetics and psychology in addition to competence in the conventions of filmmaking.

All of these concerns intersect in the problem of film's ability to produce a fictional model of the world—its mimetic quality. Cognitive psychology now tells us that we perceive the real world through "frames of representation" made up of our previous experience, our acculturation within a given socio-historical context, and our learned strategies for dealing with unfamiliar information or situations. Thus "objective reality" will appear different to people of different cultures, classes, and historical moments. The spectator's ability to "read" a feature film depends, additionally, upon a familiarity with intertextual frames: a knowledge of film language at its present point of development, of film genres perhaps, an appreciation for a given director's previous work, an understanding of the narrative conventions of fiction films.

The most subtle film directors have always taken issue with the mimetic aspect of film, and some of the best of them have exploited to the fullest the paradox of cinema: at the same time that it has a photographic relation to reality, film is a discourse, sometimes a personal vision, but in any case never more than a *version* of the reality of which it purports to be the representation. Narrative films which call attention to their status as texts tend to subvert the spectator's impression of the reliability and authority of the film narrator, and thus constitute cinematic contributions to what the French writer Nathalie Sarraute has called the "age of suspicion."

Representation, which gives back to society an image of itself, is of course one of the oldest functions of art. Like the religious ritual with which it has often been associated, art reinforces a structure of beliefs that defines and limits the possibilities of identity in an otherwise chaotic and random universe. From the earliest drawings of stone age cave dwellers to today's computerized special effects in film, the mimetic impulse has been one of the great forces in human society.

Some of the Greek myths surrounding artistic production have to do with the skill of the artist in making his representation lifelike. The artist whose work comes to life resembles a god. Pygmalion the sculptor created a woman so lifelike that she descended from her pedestal and became his wife; Orpheus the singer so charmed the rulers of the Underworld with his song that he was permitted to bring his wife Eurydice back from the dead (he lost her again when he turned and looked at her). The French critic André Bazin argued that film was capable of fulfilling the ancient dream of an art that was so true to life it could barely be distinguished from the real thing (today he would be writing about holography).

The recent philosophical discourse on representation has taken an interesting in the writings of Michel Foucault and Harold Bloom. Foucault has shown ny given moment in history a society functions within a mental set (he episteme," from the Greek word for knowledge) that affects personal litical life, the artistic as well as the economic sphere. It is no rgues, that Renaissance perspective in painting coincided with rnment in Europe. Both are organized forms that depend on in Renaissance painting, all the lines of the canvas are organized m a single point: that of the spectator, who is therefore the

ed that there is a constant tension between the artist's own e work of his or her predecessors, what he calls the "anxiety is is as true for the artist who professes "realism," as it is for eates abstract art or who tries to express inner states of mind. within the inherited traditions of culture and must wrest ori- dialogue with their precursors.

o chapters concern themselves with two films that problematize represenation. The first, on Ettore Scola's *La Nuit de Varennes*, ucauldian perspective to discuss the way that film explores different of storytelling. On the surface, the film is a fictionalized account of the ight of Louis XVI from Paris in the aftermath of the French Revolution. Scola makes this event into a parable for the epistemic shift that accompanied, as well as caused, the Revolution. The decline of hierarchy and authority consummated in Louis's fall was accompanied by similar shifts in the social concept of the self and in the conventions of storytelling. Scola casts his argument in both literary and cinematic terms and shows how all these issues are interrelated. On the one hand, he includes three famous writers among his characters, each of whom exemplifies a mode of storytelling; and on the other hand, the film uses visual quotes from the history of perspective painting and from protocinematic devices such as the peepshow to demonstrate the changed status of the subject in relation to the "authoritative" text. The three writers who appear as protagonists play out the shift from the officially sanctioned art of the court to popular art. Ultimately, the filmmaker Ettore Scola makes his case for film as the heir to literature in modern times.

The second chapter takes a more Bloomian approach and focuses on François Truffaut's anguished questioning of his cinematic muse in *La Chambre verte* (*The Green Room*). Truffaut's concerns are shown to include both the aesthetic value of cinematic representation—its ability to reproduce life despite the un-avoidable fact of death—and the place of his own work in relation to his predecessor and mentor, Jean Cocteau. *La Chambre verte* is Truffaut's own eloquent statement about the value of film art as a mode of representation, and his homage to Cocteau.

CHAPTER

3

FORMS OF REPRESENTATION
IN *LA NUIT DE VARENNES*

In *La Nuit de Varennes* Ettore Scola calls into question the mode of classical representation in film. Scola achieves this on many levels. On the one hand, he has created a self-consciously classical film on the order of Velázquez' famous Renaissance painting "Las Meninas," a painting in which the artist has represented himself at work painting the figures of the King and Queen of Spain (Fig. 9). Scola, too, has made the equivalent of a filmic self-portrait. We don't actually see the director in the film, but we become aware of the presence of the arranger through a foregrounding of the filmic apparatus. Yet Scola goes further than Velázquez: he makes a film about the impossibility of continuing the classical system. He achieves this by a mise-en-scène of various forms of storytelling that exhibit a whole panoply of narrator-narratee (storyteller to audience) relationships; and he chooses as a setting the moment of the deposition of a *political* authority—the end of the monarchy in France. The film is an Italian-French coproduction dating from 1982 which is loosely structured around the flight of Louis XVI (Louis Capet) from Paris in June of 1792 and his arrest the next day in Varennes. As in Velázquez' painting, the King and Queen are thus literally present to stand in for the representation of authority. In the remarks that follow, I will make much of the fact that the French philosopher Michel Foucault chose the Velázquez painting for his study of the whole "mind-set" of classical representation; and I will show how Scola uses his own questioning of the classical mode to characterize our modern era of uncertainty.

I begin, therefore, by imagining two moments in this film as paintings in motion: cinematic modern-day versions of Velázquez' "Las Meninas." The first moment is this: unseen by the monarchs and unseeing, since she can only hear their voices in the chamber where they are being held captive, the Countess de la Borde participates in Louis Capet's double decapitation: first by the agency of her look (she can see the bodies of the sovereigns, but not their heads); and secondly by her hearing the king read aloud the decree of the General Assembly: "En France il n'y a plus de roi"—France has a king no more. The partial

9. Diego Velázquez de Silva, *Las Meninas*. 1656. Oil on canvas, 125″ × 118 ½″; Museo del Prado, Madrid

view afforded the film spectator through the countess's point of view underscores Louis's severance from the right to represent the state. Voice and presence are henceforth dissociated.

The second moment occurs just afterward in the room into which the countess and her hairdresser, accompanied by Thomas Paine and the French chronicler and author of *Les Nuits de Paris*, Restif de la Bretonne, have retired. Here the countess is first recomposed by her servant into the fitting representation of a courtier, a process during which she looks out toward us and through the framing doorway as though at a mirror. Yielding to the pressure of Restif's insistent curiosity, she agrees to reveal the contents of the two packages that she has brought with her on the trip, packages that he himself helped to carry for her at the Tuileries as she was departing. It is before another mirror, one integral to the diegetic space this time, that the parcels are unpacked to expose the garments that, taken together, represent the authority of the king. But they are now separated from him by time (the monarch wore this cloak of majesty at a military review in Cherbourg but is in no position to do so now) and space (the room where the garments are draped on a tailor's dummy effectively cuts is off from the space of his royal representation). In the process of clothing mmy, the hairdresser presents each piece reverently to the two men and creen spectator who occupies the place of the king's subjects, a place filled.

place, for one last time, steps the countess; a point-of-view shot her glance momentarily obscures everything surrounding the nd bathes them in light. This metadiegetic moment (for nothing space motivates the change in lighting) assures our identification ess and hence our shared sorrow at the loss reenacted by this countess's last word and reverence—"Majesté"—we cut to the the film. This takes place on the bank of the Seine where Venetian manipulate a peepshow (one of the ancestors of cinema) depicting ng of Louis. These are the same storytellers that framed the film's with a recounting of the events from 1789 to 1792 that led up to the ght. But by now we have "cut away" to the 20th Century: Restif de la onne, the onlooker, climbs the stairs leading up from the quai de la Seine into the modern world of automobiles and pedestrian traffic. Scola's historical narrative foregrounds the perspective it has had all along, the perspective of the present. The viewer is left with the startling realization that it is now up to him or her to reexamine all the dialogue and events of the film in terms of the film's surprise ending.

This task is made all the more urgent by the fact that the "historical" events Scola presents, other than the attempted escape of the king, are largely invented: in the course of the film we are witness to the encounter, in a stagecoach plying its scheduled trip from Paris to Metz, of several writers and travelers: the aforementioned Thomas Paine, the French popular writer Nicholas Edmé Restif de la Bretonne, and the Chevalier de Seingalt, otherwise known as Casanova. Such an encounter is purely fictitious: according to their own published accounts, Paine and Restif remained in Paris during the king's flight, while Casanova was in Bavaria. The same liberty is taken with historical fact: Louis was not deposed at Varennes, but returned as king, as Restif describes in *Les Nuits de Paris*. What Scola dramatizes are the sentiments surrounding that return and the long-range effects of Louis's flight, with, to be sure, the hindsight of history.

In *La Nuit de Varennes* Scola expresses the nostalgia for the classical world which the king's flight irrevocably leaves behind. Flight compromises the king's authority, even if he is not immediately deposed. Scola enacts what Foucault, in *The Order of Things*, describes as the representational system of classical order at the moment when the possibility of that order is lost.

The moment of loss is dramatized in the final reverence of the countess before the symbolic garments of the king. Our understanding of this scene can profit from a juxtaposition with Michel Foucault's meditation on *Las Meninas*, the Velázquez painting he takes as the embodiment of classical representation. Many of the elements Foucault discerns in the Velázquez painting are present in this scene, though in a dynamic form. It is as though we were witness to the moment in which classical order itself comes apart, in the transition from classicism to modernism.

For Foucault this painting is emblematic of classical representation because its perspective converges on a single point, which is that of the absent sovereign. In *Las Meninas* Velázquez paints himself painting the king and queen, who are seen only as a distant mirror reflection on the wall behind him. The subject of the painting's title refers to the Infanta and her retinue who are shown in the foreground of the painting, looking out toward the regents and toward us, the viewers. In the background, a courtier appears framed against an open doorway, on the threshold of the room.

For the purposes of my argument it is important that the "absent presence" in the Velázquez painting is filled by three figures, at once subject and object, each of whom can easily substitute for the other in what Foucault describes as "a never-ending flicker"—the sovereigns, the painter (who, since he paints himself, is looking at himself as model), and the spectator who stands in the sovereigns' place. What Scola will do in this scene is to decompose that unity into its components, to substitute self-conscious presence, foregrounding (and hence undermining) in quick succession the apparatus, the spectator, and narrative authority.

In Scola's scene, we begin at the position of the courtier at the right hand of the Velázquez portrait, as the countess looks out of the framed doorway as though into a mirror. We see her reflecting herself in us, the spectators, as she is composed into the shape of a courtier, the subject of the king's authority. Her final moments as the king's subject will henceforth be ours, through the processes of filmic identification.

It is in the dynamic nature of the film medium that the courtier, who in the painting remains on the threshold, about to enter the room, does enter; the countess traverses the "mirror," bringing us as spectators empathically into the diegetic space (her place in the doorway is filled by her hairdresser) so that from an initial position of looking *at* her, we are now looking *with* her.

On screen left, Paine and Restif occupy the position of Velázquez in the painting; but where the painter looks out toward the space of the subject (be it the sovereigns, the spectators, or the painter himself), Paine looks offscreen toward the countess as though to probe the effect of the ceremony in which her servant first presents and then composes the king's robes. Without ever relinquishing our identification with the countess, we now also identify with

Paine's look *at* her: we see ourselves looking at ourselves. Paine's look toward her provides a stand-in for the spectator within the diegesis. Thus, we see ourselves looking at what she sees, which is the spectacle of the king's robes. Yet, if with the countess we see them whole, as the totalizing representation of authority, we cannot help but notice that a mirror behind the servant doubles the image in which each piece is parceled out and presented as a fragmented vestige. The wholeness that the countess sees is thus shown to be an illusion, an amalgamation of separate parts.

In the "look" exchanged between the image of the clothed king and the countess, Scola reverses the classical system in which all things converge on the represented but absent presence; separated from the symbols of his authority, the king is instead a present absence. He is present only in the imagination of the countess who calls him into being. The film arranger participates in this game of illusions by staging a shot-counter-shot between the hallucinating countess and the tailor's dummy. The countess imagines the dummy bathed in light. This light is entirely subjective, and therefore fulfills the opposite function of the light that streams in on the scene painted by Velázquez, and which underscores its codes of realism.[2] This king is presently invisible to all but her. The astonishment of the countess (and her exclamation, "Majesté") puts her in the role of the infanta of the Velázquez painting for whom the king is truly the sort of "bon papa" the French people are on the verge of repudiating.

Where then is the camera corresponding to the painter's brush, palette, and scaffolding? In fact the apparatus of cinema is everywhere present in this scene: in the metadiegetic lighting that disturbs the film's prevalent realism, in Paine's glance at the offscreen space, in the exchange of "looks" between the dummy king and the countess, as an over-the-shoulder shot of the clothed dummy toward her registers a spectacle the real king cannot see. Scola seems to say that the modern viewing experience necessitates a self-consciousness in the apparatus. In the scene immediately preceding the one I have just described, the voice-off of the imperfectly seen monarch becomes the object of the countess's and the spectator's desire to see more, opening up what Marie-Claire Ropars has called a "fissure in the enunciation." We long to see the figure of the king actually speaking the words that we hear, in the manner of classical cinema. As Ropars explains, "excluded, the synchronous voice becomes the object of desire and the bearer or factor of negation: desire of presence, a match between the voice that is heard and the being who is perceived."[3] The pathos of this scene, the sense of nostalgia it conveys, lies in our realization that the voice has forever separated from the person, who will never again speak as king. No longer able to determine events, the king will be determined by what others say about him; it is the dawn of the age of scribblers like Restif who will impose their own narrative point of view on the perception of history.

Scola has marshalled the cinematic apparatus to produce a mise-en-scène of the modern separation of the subject from classical representation, and he has chosen the very moment at which this separation was first made. Consciously

10. Decline of the classical narrative's powers of seduction (Marcello Mastroianni as Casanova). (Ettore Scola, *La Nuit de Varennes*)

or not, he has also chosen one of the natural subjects of cinema. The story-telling capacities of the stagecoach travelers enable him to explore various other ways of positioning the subject in narrative, turning *La Nuit de Varennes* into a parable for the forces that determined the emergence of modernity.

The three positions Scola explores are exemplified by Thomas Paine, Restif de la Bretonne, and Casanova. Among these, that of Casanova is perhaps the most interesting, because the treatment of him parallels that of the king; it is as though he were the king's feminine image. Scola presents us with an aging lover whose body and voice are decaying (Fig. 10). To the beautiful widow who spontaneously offers herself to him, he replies: "It is not this old man who takes your breath away, but his name, his reputation, his past. All that which today exists no more." Casanova's is a fragmented body, onto which he grafts the vestiges of representation for the sake of that story which is his past. His costume is not the cloak of royal authority but the accoutrement of seduction: braided coat, make-up kit ("le nécessaire"), and wig. The women in the stagecoach are seduced by the story he represents, which is the story of desire and seduction itself. So he plies his way through the world, dropping aphorisms as he goes; this is the Casanova of the memoirs, and not one whom any of the travelers would have been in a position to know. Scola makes of this lover in his twilight years the very embodiment of the classical narrative that will experience an eclipse in modern times. Here too the feeling is one of nostalgia, as the aging pleaser makes a charming case for a type of storytelling that is now outmoded.[4]

Anyone who has looked into Casanova's memoirs must be struck, I think, by the way in which they dramatize what Ross Chambers has called "narrative seduction."[5] In tale after tale the writer explains how fate and circumstances deprived him of the company of the woman whose favor he had won; unlike the myth of Don Juan which posits the subjection of woman by man, Casanova's success with women consists in conversation and identification with her.[6] In the film as well, Casanova is always the seduced rather than the seducer, Mastroianni sending back to the spectator the mirror of his or her own stance as seduced narratee. The persona the writer of the memoirs presents is that of a naive and sincere lover continually thwarted by the wicked world of husbands, political authorities, and jealous rivals.[7] Scola follows this suggestion, making Casanova into an object of desire, more stereotypically feminine than masculine; a radical student scornfully addresses him as "Madame Casanova." Restif's first look at him parallels the typical mode of filming women in Hollywood melodramas who have undergone a "feminine metamorphosis"; the camera starts at the shoes, then moves up to catalogue the successive charms of legs, waist, bust, and head crowned with a hat.

It is not by chance that Scola chooses Casanova as the personification of classical storytelling. He exhibits that undivided consciousness of the classical writer who never questions his centrality to the story. Everything revolves around him; like the king in the Velázquez painting, he is the point and focus of the representation. And, although the stories appear to be about Casanova's experiences with others, they evoke the personality of the storyteller himself.

Yet just as Scola dramatizes the precise moment when political authority vacillates, there is trouble in the house of fiction as well. Casanova's repeated insistence on his failing charms and the transparency of his masquerade leave some doubt as to whether the classical mode of address is destined to last very much longer. An old man, he repeatedly nods off in mid-sentence. At one of the inn stops, his attempt to show Restif how he entertains at court is cut short by his glance at an old woman who ignores him. During this scene, the extra-diegetic music playing the catalogue of women from Mozart's *Don Giovanni* provides an ironic counterpoint to the seducer's failing powers.[8]

As though in anticipation of modernism, Scola has Casanova address us, the spectators, beyond the grave, in order to explain why his fellow travelers have not had the opportunity of reading his memoirs: "It is important to explain that my name was virtually unknown in France at this time. My very popular memoirs were not published until after my death, which took place in 1798." Scola effectively accuses Casanova of self-consciously producing his life as story. In another moment of rupture, a voice and image intrude to give a dictionary definition of a word employed by Casanova (the term "désobligeante," reserved for a type of vehicle so uncomfortable that the driver is not obliged to invite others to ride with him).

In this film about history-making and storytelling no tales are actually told; nor does anything really happen, except the *stopping* of the vehicle of the king at Varennes; arrest, rather than progress, is its master metaphor. The stories of Restif and Casanova are referred to as past seductions fondly remembered in the absence of present ones. The conversations in the stagecoach function as extradiegetic tellings of past events that exist in offscreen space; but these tellings hold the potential for seduction. Gamely, the countess urges Restif and Casanova to seduce one of the three traveling women (an opera singer and a rich widow are also among the passengers), for hasn't Restif written about more desperate situations: making love with a woman while her husband slept in the same bed, making love in a tree, in a rowboat, in a confessional, or with a girl holding the yarn for her blind mother. This offscreen space becomes identified as the locus of male narrative authority, an impression reinforced by the fact that all the asides and interruptions are spoken by male voices (this occurs even when the countess is recalling the king's appearance at Cherbourg; the explanatory note is voiced by a man). The diegetic space inside the stagecoach, on the other hand, remains the locus of what Ross Chambers calls the "narrational" where the narrator's desire to please meets the narratee's readiness to be seduced; it is also a male-dominated place, but one in which "the maintenance of narrative authority implies an act of seduction."[9] The opera singer manages to get rid of her male companion, a judge who seems uninterested in taking part in the game: he gets sent up to ride outside with the coachman so that she can listen undisturbed.

Thomas Paine is allowed to stay on as a privileged outsider. Historically, it was Paine who, upon the return of the king, placarded Paris with the manifesto of the "Société Républicaine," which argued that the king had deposed himself by his flight:

> The nation can never give back its confidence to a man who . . . conspires a clandestine flight, obtains a fraudulent passport, conceals a King of France under the disguise of a valet, directs his course towards a frontier covered with traitors and deserters . . . He holds no longer any authority. We owe him no longer obedience. We see in him no more than an indifferent person; we can regard him only as Louis Capet.[10]

Through identification with Paine, the spectator experiences the ambivalent feelings associated with the loss of the old order. It is he who gives the most rational reason for its demise: what kind of government is it, he asks, that places on the throne after a lion, an ass?[11] Yet this statement earns him the scorn of the countess, to whom he is attracted. To regain her good graces, he expresses the wish to see the traveling case in which she reverently preserves the portraits of the royal family. Thus even Paine, in Scola's account, is seduced by the force of the story that he witnesses.

La Nuit de Varennes appears to take place on a threshold. After its opening at the peepshow on the quai de la Seine, Scola cuts to Restif's press where his introduction to the French translation of Paine's *The Rights of Man* is being confiscated for non-payment of alimony. From there we shift to another liminal situation, as Restif himself is drawn over the threshold of a "maison de tolérance" by the interpellation of the Madam, an old friend. The young girl who is offered to him is herself enclosed in an alcove, and perfectly framed by a round mirror that shows her off to advantage. The way that that image refers to classical representation is underscored by Restif's exclamation that her image is "uncontestable proof of the existence of God." The lacy enclosure which contains her also echoes the peepshow that frames the story.

Restif enters that space, but stops short upon hearing that things are afoot in the palace of the Tuileries. Rushing to that scene, he meets the countess on another threshold and has the accidental opportunity of handing the mysterious package to her as she pauses on the step of the carriage that is to follow the king. The steps of the "diligence," too, are constantly in the foreground; Casanova and the countess pause on it to reflect that it is too late for love, and it is here that decisions are made as to just who will ride inside. It becomes, literally, the vehicle for the advance of the narrative. The two scenes I began by describing are also threshold scenes, framed respectively by the stair and the door. What unifies the narrative, finally, is the recurrence of liminality: in this film, it is always too late for love, too late to save the king, too late for new stories, too late for anyone to escape. What Scola has produced is a mise-en-scène of Foucault's "threshold between Classicism and modernity . . . when words ceased to intersect with representations and to provide a spontaneous grid for the knowledge of things."[12]

In this film of many transitional moments, the deposition of the king only serves as the vehicle through which the far-reaching historical effects of this change are explored. Practicing what Hayden White would call an organicist approach to history, one which makes sense out of the historical process by explaining particular events in relation to an integrated scheme of "ideas" or "principles,"[13] Scola discerns a wide variety of epistemic shifts. These include:

1. The crisis in the identity of the subject that comes with the loss of a secure ground for self-representation;

2. The transition from the authority of the voice to the instrumentality of writing as the expression of the authority of the state;

3. The rise of a class of writers and intellectuals with political influence, and the putting forth of writing, on the basis of personal experience and philosophy, as a true witness to historical events;

4. The shift of desire from signified to signifier, so that the object of desire becomes a token of exchange rather than an end pursued for its own sake.

THE CRISIS IN THE IDENTITY OF THE SUBJECT

With the fall of the king, the subject must find a new position in a political system deprived of patriarchal, monarchic, authorial presence. Here, the "sub-

11. Nostalgia for the old order (Hanna Schygulla as the Countess). (Ettore Scola, *La Nuit de Varennes*)

ject" is taken to mean not only the king's historical subjects, who lose their identity as "subjects of the crown" once he is deposed, but also the self as the subject of address in language. Fundamental changes in the order of society entail a cognitive shift in this "subject" as well.

La Nuit de Varennes can be read as a dramatization of the forces that have determined how we, as film spectators at this specific point in history, have come into being. As we pass through the different points of identification, circulating between Restif, Paine, the countess, and Casanova, we experience in a vicarious way the separation from a stable identity as subject that the fall of the king signifies. The uncertainty that befalls the countess can thus be read as the spectator's own, and Scola's repeated showing of her in the frame of doorways and windows as nostalgia for the old order (Fig. 11). She explains to Paine that the king was her ideal, her religion, her security, but that any other ideal would make her feel just as secure. Yes, answers Paine, "with our faith and our ideals we try to avoid being afraid; but we have to find ideals that are appropriate (qui nous conviennent); if we become aware that our ideals are at an impasse we have to have the courage to change them." The spectator's successive identifications with Casanova or the countess, with Restif or Thomas Paine, amount to a sort of declension of the possibility of identity. As film spectators, we are free to explore the various different positions, from classical to modernist, and to sift out the way in which this film encourages us to reenact vicariously, not just the facts of history, but schemas for historical understanding.

THE TRANSITION FROM THE AUTHORITY
OF THE VOICE TO THAT OF WRITING

Scola puts forth a cinema of writing as one step toward finding a film form more appropriate to the age; if the figures of the countess and Casanova are used as models of classical representation, the arranger interrupts their stories. Restif is presented in a more positive light. Like the medium of film today, Restif's writings were looked down upon in his own time because they were "popular." His favorite subjects were of the working class. Casanova recites the titles with delight: *The Natural Daughter, The Parisian Household, The New Abelard, Contemporary Women, The Foot of La Fanchette*. Rumor and scandal are Restif's allies as he goes about his investigations, trying to understand, to frame coherently, what he sees and overhears. His relation to reality is the dramatization of what Roland Barthes has called the "writerly" (*scriptible*). For this protojournalist, overheard conversations and rumors are texts that activate him as a "reader" to search for meaning. Restif can be understood as the prototype of the modern reader or film spectator for whom all texts are *scriptible*; indeed, as Ross Chambers has shown, an active engagement in the text has become the new condition for legibility.[14]

THE RISE OF THE CLASS
OF WRITERS AND INTELLECTUALS

Restif is the true hero of Scola's narrative, despite the fact that he also allows the spectator the pleasure of identifying with the countess and Casanova (Fig. 12). To some extent the script of the film can be considered an adaptation of Restif's own *Nuits de Paris*, in which he recounts the circumstances surrounding Louis's flight. Restif deploys the cognitive strategies the spectator must adopt to follow the mystery plot to its conclusion. This plot hinges on the mysterious package he hands to the countess, an episode taken literally from *Les Nuits de Paris*, dated April 17–18. On this day, however, Louis was prevented from leaving Paris. His real flight occurred a few months later, and Restif learned of it on the streets of Paris, as he describes in his entry of June 22–24.[15] Linking the departure of the two women to the flight of Louis, and the package to the king's royal garments, is an essential aspect of Scola's plot.

Restif is the one character of the story who is allowed the privilege of enunciating in his own voice texts that he has written: the first of these is a warning to the aristocracy in which he predicts the outbreak of the Revolution, the second a look forward to the year 1992. For the first of these, Scola chooses the mechanism of an insert with Restif looking directly at the spectator (or into

12. The writer, new hero of the modern age (Jean-Louis Barrault as Restif de la Bretonne). (Ettore Scola, *La Nuit de Varennes*)

the camera), similar to Casanova's explanatory note on his subsequent fame and death; but as he speaks he is also setting his words in type. For the second, which is also the concluding shot of the film, he returns to the quai de la Seine in front of the Venetian peepshow showing the execution of Louis XVI and Marie Antoinette.

The peepshow is commented in a manner that enables us to identify its aesthetics with those of classical narrative cinema: "a machine for seeing the world." Everything the Venetian master of ceremonies says about his show applies to classical cinema as well: "Observe with your own eyes the great events of history, where reality becomes fantasy and fantasy reality . . . Come and see the history of the world in moving images." Restif moves away from this model of storytelling as he climbs the steps away from the quai and enters the modern world. As he climbs, he recites a passage from *Les Nuits de Paris* that looks forward to the year 1992. In the passage quoted Scola has found an echo of his own organicist approach to history:

> *Les Nuits de Paris*: "These ideas exhausted me. For relief I plunged into the centuries that followed. I saw the people of 1992 reading our history. I strained to hear them and I heard. The severity of their judgement against Louis amazed me. It seemed to me that some accused him of incalculable wrongs; while others more terrible still thanked him for having been the

instrument for the destruction of royalty. All Europe apparently had a new government; but I saw on the pages of history the terrible jolts the nations had endured. I seemed to hear readers saying to each other: 'We're glad we didn't live in those terrible times, when human life counted as nothing.' One of their philosophers cried out: 'These jolts are necessary from time to time, so people appreciate peace and quiet, just as one needs sickness to value good health.' 'But' (replied one of his *confrères*), 'would you have wanted to be the jolter, or the jolted?' 'No, no, I wouldn't want to be either! But I wouldn't have minded having been either one. Once past, the pain which one has survived is pleasure.' 'Ha! you deep thinkers,' replied a visionary hidden in a corner, 'you *were* the people of 200 years ago: you are made of their organic molecules, and you are at peace, because these molecules are weary of war. You will come back to it, after a long rest . . . ' "16

This passage (which Scola does not quote in its entirety) allows the director to make the transition to the perspective of the present, and it is not without significance that he gets there by way of Restif's own writings. Writing is proposed, in this film, as the tool of historical understanding. The reader as writer, the citizen who takes upon himself the role of witness to history, are aptly characterized in Restif's own self-description: "Literary types, chroniclers, scribblers, we are a race of spies. We don't participate—we write, classify, and confuse everything. We are a curious race." Scola's visual mise-en-scène suggests that cinema may be as valid a tool for the understanding of history as the written word.

THE SHIFT OF DESIRE FROM THE SIGNIFIED TO THE SIGNIFIER

In this historical parable, the characters seem caught up in a game of chess in which they shift from king to pawn; who can take them depends on their current value of exchange. For instance Casanova is pursued for his reputation rather than for any real charms he still possesses. He is forcefully abducted at the end of the film by his patron who sends out two thugs in an armored carriage to bring him back to Bavaria; and the king is "as good as dead," as Casanova puts it, once he is taken prisoner, not by another king, but by a candle-maker. The same holds, Scola seems to say, for the subject of cinema, the spectator, in the sense that his enactment of the writerly entails a delaying play with the erotics of the cinematic gaze; just as Casanova is nothing more than the signifier of his former self, the spectator is constantly looking at looking rather than being held in an unproblematized relation with the image. Like Velázquez, Scola uses the *mise-en-abyme* to place the spectator in an unstable position, at once inside the diegetic space and outside it looking in.17

As Restif enters the modern world in the last shot of this film, he becomes one of us and urges that we search in everyday events for signals of what is to come. This final voice is the voice of writing, making writers of us all. As told by Scola, *La Nuit de Varennes* is the story of a loss, not just of the classical view of the world, but of the stability of the subject. By thinking through the implications of this loss on many levels, Scola has provided a convincing metaphor for our own restless position as film spectators.

CHAPTER

4

TRUFFAUT AND COCTEAU
Representations of Orpheus

Although Scola questions modes of storytelling and their relation to conventions of representation, the medium of film is no source of anxiety to him. It is different for François Truffaut in *La Chambre verte* (*The Green Room*), a film made in 1978. Here the artist questions not only his own role as artist but also the ability of the film medium to represent anything lifelike. This is a work that stands as a testimonial to Truffaut's conception of the art of film, and of his own role as artist.

La Chambre verte is Truffaut's most philosophical film. In it he reflected on his creative sources as a filmmaker, consciously quoting artists like Jean Cocteau and Abel Gance who had influenced him in his early career. He also quoted extensively from his own previous films (especially *L'Enfant sauvage*). Finally, he wove into his adaptation of three stories by Henry James ("The Green Room," "The Beast in the Jungle," and "The Friends of the Friends") a discourse on the relation between art, life, and death. Truffaut's ambitious scope places the film alongside other works, both literary and cinematic, that have struggled with the same themes: the films of Cocteau, the writings of Edgar Allan Poe, Villiers de l'Isle Adam, and Italo Calvino. The depth of his insights makes it appropriate to draw on the critical writings of Harold Bloom, which can help to elucidate the complex textual strategies that Truffaut has resorted to in his film.

At the turning point of *La Chambre verte*, the bereaved Julien Davenne, who is still mourning the loss of his wife eleven years ago, orders the destruction of a wax model he had had made of her (Fig. 13). The offended artist protests in vain that the lifesized doll is exactly like the photograph Davenne gave him as a model. Davenne refuses what he calls the "thing"; he won't recognize any connection between it and his beloved Julie. Most especially, he cannot bear her look—the way her eyes stare blankly out into space. Before the artist begins his act of destruction, the point of view shifts abruptly to a position in the darkness outside the brightly-lit studio; through the window, the artist is seen dismantling the likeness of Julie with the blows of an axe. The spectator is

13. The unsatisfactory representation (François Truffaut as Julien Davenne). (François Truffaut, *La Chambre vert*)

doubly implicated in this assassination of representation, which is experienced at once from the position of that lurking, voyeuristic camera, and from the darkened perspective of the movie theater. In the larger context of the film, this "murder" of the woman's image becomes the figure for Truffaut's questioning of cinematic representation.

In despair, Davenne returns to the cemetery where a photographic medallion adorns Julie's tombstone—the same pose that he keeps enshrined in his home. As he stands before the tomb, the photograph becomes the starting point for his reverie. The camera pans down to the inscription "Julie Davenne née Valence 1897–1919." The last visitors to the cemetery leave, and the guardian closes the gates, leaving Davenne locked inside for the night. Davenne is now shut into a separate space devoted to the dead, a fact that Truffaut underscores by accompanying the hero's suspension in thought with music that evokes the visit to the underworld in Jean Cocteau's *Orphée* (1950). In Cocteau's film the poet and his guide traverse a mirror in search of the poet's deceased wife Eurydice. They penetrate into "the Zone" where the dead walk around repeating the gestures they have made in life. It is a place, Cocteau writes, "made up of men's memories and the ruins of their habits."[1]

With a characteristic economy of means, Truffaut accomplishes a number of things with this intertextual musical quotation. The first is the temporary suspension of diegetic time which would be unequivocal to viewers familiar with *Orphée*—in the "Zone," there is no time. Truffaut implicitly suggests that the deceased can be kept alive by memory, a memory which, in this case, is transmitted by a photograph. Here the filmmaker reopens the whole question of the relation of photography to death, memory, and the passage of time, about which there is a significant body of literature, from the writings of Siegfried Kracauer and Walter Benjamin to Roland Barthes. Secondly, the placement of the photograph among competing forms of representation that appear in the film (such as the wax model) raises the question of the relation of cinema itself to life and death, a question taken up as early as 1945 by Truffaut's mentor André Bazin in his essay, "The Ontology of the Photographic Image." The choice of the most efficient vehicle for returning the dead to life is a theme to be found, moreover, not only in the Henry James stories upon which Truffaut constructs his tale, but in the writings of Edgar Allan Poe ("The Oval Portrait"), Villiers de l'Isle Adam ("Véra"), and Italo Calvino (*Invisible Cities*).

As a myth that enacts the origin of art, the Orpheus story is one that Truffaut appropriately cites. In Greek mythology, Orpheus was the musician who managed to wrest his wife Eurydice from the powers of Hades (the underworld where spirits went after death) by charming the gods with his lyre. The gods stipulated that he could have her back on condition that he would not turn and look at her on his way back to earth. At a fatal moment, Orpheus fell victim to his curiosity and turned, thus losing Eurydice forever. The French critic Maurice Blanchot has argued that Orpheus's decision to turn and look at Eurydice embodies that which is most at stake in art: the necessity to create life out of death, while at the same time consigning that life back to its inert origins in order to validate the artist.[2] Edgar Allan Poe wrestled with the problem in "The Oval Portrait" (1842), the story of a painter whose portrait of his wife is so lifelike that it replaces the original—he paints the life right out of her, and she dies even as he applies the final brushstroke. In Poe's ironic twist on the Orpheus tale, the artist has thus brought his beloved back from the dead even before she is deceased—only to lose her *because* of his art. Villiers de L'Isle Adam makes more traditional use of the myth in "Véra" (1874). There, the bereaved husband conjures up his departed wife by arranging things in their bedroom so that she still appears to live there. When she finally appears, he loses her again by exclaiming "But you are dead!"

Davenne's initial strategy is similar to that of Villiers's hero. In a room of his house ("the green room" of the title), he has carefully preserved relics of Julie: a model cast of Julie's hand, a ring that belonged to her and which is molded into the symbol of infinity, as well as photographs and portraits. But the room is struck by lightning and Davenne has to rescue the precious relics from the flames.

It is while leaving the cemetery after his reverie that Davenne finds the solution to preserving the memory of his beloved. On his way out, he comes upon a chapel abandoned since the war (we are in the year 1930). He chooses this site as a place to honor the dead, *his* dead, as he puts it—those who have meant something to him. Around Julie's photograph he now puts up others.

From James's story "The Altar of the Dead," Truffaut took the idea of the altar lit by candles, where each candle represents one of the hero's dead friends. The photographs are an addition to the story, as is Davenne's employment as a journalist whose main talent is writing obituaries. Another addition is the deaf and dumb child whom Davenne has adopted. The child becomes another symbol of Davenne's devotion to the dead, in line with James's suggestion that the dead are dumb, though still present ("They were there in their simplified essence, their conscious expressive patience, as personally there as if they had only been stricken dumb"). With this child, he looks at slides of soldiers killed during the First World War, a war in which the hero lost many of his friends.

At the auction of his deceased wife's family estate, Davenne meets a young woman, Cecilia, who is instrumental in helping him secure Julie's ring. It happens that they knew each other as children, during an archeological expedition to Pompeii. Instead of falling in love with her, Julien converts her to his cult of the dead, and introduces her to the chapel. Although the circumstance of their meeting is Truffaut's addition, their relationship finds echoes in three stories by James. In "The Friends of the Friends," the narrator breaks off her engagement when she realizes that her fiancé is visited nightly by the ghost of a female friend (again, the ghost is said to be "dumb"); like Cecilia in Truffaut's story, this friend had, during her lifetime, been visited by the ghost of her father at the time of his death. In "The Beast in the Jungle," a man passes up a passionate relationship with a woman (whom he had also met at Pompeii some sixteen years earlier), only to realize after her death that to have loved her would have given meaning to his otherwise wasted life. And in "The Altar of the Dead," the relationship between the two friends never blossoms into romance; James strongly suggests that the fault was the man's, who failed to love life more than death.

Having secured in Cecilia an interlocutor for Julien, Truffaut strides into the heart of a mystery. For he has the hero invent stories about the people depicted on the wall, stories intended to convey to Cecilia a pathos so that she too will be able to identify with his loss. The mystery comes from the fact that while the photographs are those of people that no doubt meant much to Truffaut the filmmaker, the stories are completely invented (remember that we are in the year 1930, two years before Truffaut was born). Davenne tells a story about each of Truffaut's friends, whose death is represented as occurring before the birth of the artist. One should bear in mind as well that the film audience could not be expected to know the real identity of all the authors, musicians, and filmmakers reproduced in the photographs. Ostensibly Truffaut's purpose was something other than paying homage to his dead friends; some of the people depicted were still very much alive in 1978 when the film came out.

Passing in front of a photo of Raymond Queneau and Janine Queneau (Fig. 14) Davenne says:

14. Photographic representation and death. (François Truffaut, *La Chambre verte*)

They married in 1911, and during three years they were never separated, not for a day, not for an hour; and when he was called up by the army, she wanted to throw herself out the window; the neighbors prevented her. So he deserted in order to come back to her because he could no more do without her than she without him. They managed to reach Holland where they died, not long ago, a few years, a few days apart, like siamese twins.

The only true part of this story is the fact that Queneau (1908–1976) did not outlive his wife Janine (whom he married in 1928 after completing his military service in 1927) by more than a few years. Of Oscar Lewenstein, coproducer of Truffaut's *The Bride Wore Black*: "His name was Simon Jardine. He came from Ireland. During the 30 years he spent in our region the police and the courts had very little work. His reputation for honesty and logic was such that people who had disagreements preferred to have their conflicts resolved by him."[3] As he comments on the photographs of Oscar Werner (who played in *Jules and Jim* and *Fahrenheit 451*), Maurice Jaubert (whose music accompanies many of the scenes of this film), and Henry James, Davenne continues to tell stories. The point seems to be that the photograph cannot mean anything without the story that explains it.

Roland Barthes makes a similar point in *Camera lucida*, where he describes his search for that photograph of his mother which will best represent what she was for him. Having found it, he refuses to reproduce it for the reader; its special meaning, poignancy, *punctum* as he calls it, signifies only for him. He realizes that henceforth he must "interrogate the evidence of Photography, not from the viewpoint of pleasure, but in relation to what we romantically call Love and Death."[4] Walter Benjamin, too, who wrote a famous essay on the modern art work's loss of aura through mechanical reproduction, was aware of the aura that a photograph can have;[5] even though it is a reproduction to the extent that the idea of the "original" is not as strong as it is in painting, a photograph is the record of a specific moment in time. For this reason, an old photograph often conjures up an experience of the uncanny, the return of the familiar in the guise of the strange. This is what Barthes calls its *spectrum*. With the passage of time, the photograph of a person assumes the configuration of his or her history: under the photograph of a person, writes Siegfried Kracauer, the history of a human being is buried as under a cover of snow.[6]

A photograph functions in relation to a viewer; it is the starting point for a memory image. When Barthes discovers that a childhood photograph of his mother is in fact what he has been looking for all along, he has discovered what Kracauer calls her "monogram," her best memory image.[7]

This is to say that photographs do not signify by themselves; perhaps more strongly than other texts and images, because apparently more removed from the vicissitudes of textuality, they underscore the intertextual nature of the construction of meaning. "It is not the human being that stands out from his photograph," writes Kracauer, "but the sum of what can be subtracted from him . . . people's traits are contained solely in their 'history.' "[8]

What Davenne does with his narration is to construct a meaning for each picture—no matter that this is not the meaning that the photograph has for Truffaut himself (or for that matter, for any film spectator who may recognize the identity of the persons represented). Each is surrounded by a narrative.

Truffaut's preference for narrative becomes clearer once we realize that his film is filled with multiple references to other filmmakers and to his own work. This was the third of Truffaut's films in which he himself appeared in a major role. As Doctor Itard in *L'Enfant sauvage* (1969) he becomes the teacher of a deaf and dumb child who has grown up in the wild. His relationship with the child has some parallels to that of Davenne with the deaf and dumb youngster of *La Chambre verte*. Davenne's obsession with preserving the memory of loved ones echoes the preservation of books by memorization in *Fahrenheit 451* (1966); and his obsessive love of Julie recalls the obsession of Victor Hugo's daughter in *L'Histoire d'Adèle H* (1975). The slides he looks at with his foster son recall the slide show in *Jules et Jim* (1961). And the film looks forward to Truffaut's subsequent work as well: The initial title of the film, *La Disparue*, is the title of the play that Marion Steiner is performing in *Le Dernier métro* (1980).

The Cocteau quotations abound. Some of these are as subtle as a choice of style. When the young boy sneaks out at night, he is reflected by mirrors in the stairwell that recall the mirrors used in *Orphée* as entry into the "Zone." The deserted street seems a timeless no-man's land, much like Cocteau's visualization of the underworld. Another mirror shot later in the film shows Davenne speaking to the doctor. The shot implies that Julien is already, somehow, "on the other side" or soon to be going there (in fact he dies shortly thereafter). The cemetery itself appears as a kind of "Zone." A direct quotation occurs during the interrogation of Cecilia by Davenne's boss. He says "Je crois que vous aimez cet homme," a line from Cocteau's judges of the underworld; and he sits, like Cocteau's judges, before the accused.

Finally, the filmmaker pays tribute to his own history as a film viewer. Truffaut has said that his first awareness of the power of cinema to move an audience occurred at the projection of Abel Gance's 1936 film *Paradis perdu*.[9] In this film, a man commemorates his dead wife's love by preserving mementos of their past in alcoves that look like little stages. At the end of the film, he gives up the idea of marriage to a young woman so that his daughter (who looks like her mother) can marry the man she loves. From his experience of this film, Truffaut may have taken the germ of the idea for *La Chambre verte*. Quotations of other filmmakers are in abundance. A shot of Davenne driving home in the rain quotes a shot from Hitchcock's *Psycho* (Truffaut wrote a book on Hitchcock, whose influence on his style has been exhaustively studied).[10]

The most obvious intertext in the film seems to be the work of Cocteau. The presence of Cocteau is so strong that one suspects Truffaut of making this film in part to repay a long-standing debt to his predecessor. It was Cocteau who introduced Truffaut to Bazin, and Truffaut in his younger days was equally influenced by both. Eugene P. Walz has noted the influence of Cocteau's style on Truffaut's short story "Antoine et l'orpheline," written in 1955.[11] Truffaut also honored Cocteau in an essay appearing in the *Cahiers du cinéma* in 1954, for being one of the first French cinematic "authors."[12] A poster advertising Cocteau's *Le Testament d'Orphée* (*The Testament of Orpheus*, 1959) appears in Truffaut's *La Peau douce* (*The Soft Skin*, 1964).

The very fact that Truffaut achieves his effects through the devices of intertextuality suggests the terms of Harold Bloom's *The Anxiety of Influence*; if *La Chambre verte* derives some of its hidden power from *Orphée*, in the manner of the "return of the dead" that Bloom calls *apophrades*, it also participates in its own "erasure," since Truffaut imposes on himself a voluntary asceticism and paucity of means. This *askesis*, to retain the Bloomian figure, is consistent with the orphic theme itself, which mythically and historically is characterized by an ascetic philosophy. In the Greek myth, Orpheus was punished by Dionysus for defecting to the cult of Apollo. He was torn to pieces by the Maenads. The cult of Orphism in Greek times was characterized by vegetarianism, sexual abstention, and other austerities.[13]

Truffaut's relation to Cocteau's work in this film is a combination of two of the figures that Bloom has described in his attempt to trace the relation between major literary figures and their precursors. Basically, he argues that a strong poet inevitably has to wrestle with the influence of an important precursor. The struggle is always reflected in the new poet's work. The result of Truffaut's struggle with Cocteau is very much present in *La Chambre verte*; indeed the presence of Cocteau in this film is one of the elements that makes this a "film about film."

In the preface to *The Films in My Life* Truffaut writes that as a filmmaker he demands that "a film express either the *joy of making cinema* or *the agony of making cinema.*"[14] Truffaut's earlier film about the making of a movie, *La Nuit américaine* (*Day for Night*, 1973), reflected some of the joy. Read as a film about film, *La Chambre verte* is more nearly about the anxiety (Truffaut's own word was "angoisse," or anguish). What one reviewer called the "morbid, unpleasant *The Green Room*"[15] is the site of a struggle between Truffaut and his predecessor Cocteau, a struggle for self-definition and identity on the part of Truffaut that takes place on the difficult terrain of the filmmaker's own relation to life, art, and death.[16]

To return to Bloom's description of *apophrades*: this is the term he gives to that relation between a poet and a predecessor when "the new poem's achievement makes it seem to us, not as though the precursor were writing it, but as though the later poet himself had written the precursor's characteristic work."[17] It is as though, Bloom later writes, the earlier poet had at last found his true voice in the later.

In *La Chambre verte* Davenne speaks of "finishing off the figure" ("achever la figure") by his own death—his array of candles will then be complete. And, unlike the James stories in which the male protagonists are all still living at the end, Davenne dies in the final moments of the film. The corpus of works Bloom invites us to imagine (a corpus in which this film would figure as the last of Cocteau's films, just as Cocteau's films would seem to have been filmed by Truffaut) is then complete.

There are difficulties in transposing Bloom's terms to the cinema, if only because the visual style of a Cocteau or a Truffaut is so clearly that of its author. Yet in some ways *La Chambre verte* is Truffaut's "remake" of Cocteau's *Le Testament d'Orphée* (*The Testament of Orpheus*), a film made in 1960, three years before Cocteau's death, and for which the young Truffaut was the co-producer. Truffaut's film, like Cocteau's, is made with the idea of leaving a legacy to the future. This legacy, while paying homage to the artists' original sources of inspiration, addresses itself to the ultimate question for the artist: that of the importance of his art, the reason for his choosing art as his life's work.

The idea of leaving a legacy for future generations of artists was Cocteau's avowed reason for making the *Le Testament d'Orphée*. The Princess of Death comes back to question her maker Cocteau. What is film? she asks. Cocteau answers that film is "a spring that crystallizes thoughts . . . A film brings back to life our actions which have died. Film lends to the unreal the appearance of reality." Dedication to art is worth dying for in *Le Testament d'Orphée*; at the end the poet is killed by the lance thrown by Minerva (Athena), the goddess of wisdom. Cocteau (who, like Truffaut, appears in the main role in his own film) demonstrates that the poet pays with his own life for his dedication to art. Truffaut does no less, ending his film with a mise-en-scène of Davenne's last gasp. Yet in both films there is a joy in this self-immolation, an embracing of the poet's fate that amounts to a celebration of the self. Truffaut's film is a return to Cocteau's themes, but one that stands proudly on the achievements of a lifetime. As Bloom writes, "*apophrades*, when managed by the capable imagination, by the strong poet who has persisted in his strength, becomes not so much a return of the dead as a celebration of the return of the early self-exaltation that first made poetry possible."[18]

I have said that the relationship between Cocteau and Truffaut in this film is also one of *askesis* or asceticism. Bloom writes that in this type of relation, the later poet undergoes a voluntary impoverishment of his own means of expression and thereby strips the precursor of his endowment.[19] We may opt to read this film as a subtle warning against the substitution of art for life, a self-criticism of Truffaut's that implicitly accuses Cocteau as well.

Italo Calvino, in *Invisible Cities*, imagined a city doubled by a ghastly underworld. In Eusapia, the dead are transported to an identical subterranean copy of the city where they continue their former activities.[20] In the end, the inhabitants cannot tell which is the city of the living and which is the city of the dead. Taken as an allegory of cinema, Calvino's story suggests the danger that real life may become a second-hand experience dominated by our concern for how it fits our conventional representations of reality.

Truffaut has curtailed Cocteau's vision by excluding from his film any visual representation of the uncanny, the ghostlike (he has also remarkably transformed James's stories, published under the title "Tales of the Supernatural"). In the visual look of his film, he has turned his back on the surrealist devices that are Cocteau's constant resource in *Orphée*. For instance, one of the most obvious intertexts to Cocteau's film is that of the surrealist paintings of Giorgio de Chirico. De Chirico's urban landscapes were celebrated by Breton and other surrealists for their ability to suggest the uncanny, the feeling of the return of something that had been repressed in the viewer's unconscious. The brightly lit but bare exteriors look strangely like interiors; they are populated by red gloves, monumental artichokes, disembodied shadows—a series of recurring objects whose juxtaposition seems to hover at the edge of meaning. The paintings he did in 1913–14, such as "The Anxious Journey" (Fig. 15) and "The Song of Love" (Fig. 16), when seen in conjunction with *Orphée*, enable the spectator to reframe the film in terms of surrealist imagery, even though Cocteau himself was never an official member of the movement.[21] The glove that the princess wears in order to traverse the mirror, and that Orpheus appropriates, recalls the one which occurs in many of these paintings, and the script specifies that it should be a red glove; Breton had reproduced "The Enigma of Fate" with its bright red glove in his first surrealist novel, *Nadja* (1928). In particular, there are scenes that seem largely inspired by the mood that permeates de Chirico's urban landscapes. In one of these Orphée vainly pursues the princess through

15. Giorgio de Chirico, *The Anxious Journey.* 1913. Oil on canvas, 29 ¼" × 42";
Collection, The Museum of Modern Art, New York. Acquired through the
Lillie P. Bliss Bequest.

the deserted streets of Paris, from Montmartre to Les Halles to the Place
Vendôme (Fig. 17). The rapid editing translates him instantly from one distant
place to another. The sense of emptiness, of anxiety, seems translated from
the paintings onto film, as though Cocteau had found in the arcades of the Place
Vendôme the representation of something he remembered from de Chirico's
paintings. The same may be said of the film's final shot in which Heurtebise
and the princess are taken to their doom (Fig. 18).[22]

Against the exuberance of Cocteau's surrealist style, Truffaut imposes strict,
ascetic limitations to expression: his own atonal speech, his wooden acting style,
the monochrome effect of what is supposedly a color film. Ironically, all these
devices which make the spectator conscious of the cinematic apparatus end up
highlighting the power of that cinema. Despite the laying bare of filmic devices,
we remain involved in the narrative. The foregrounding of the apparatus necessarily brings us back to the still photograph, that unit of meaning that filmic
perception occludes. As Stephen Heath writes: "Made of a series of stops in
time, the timed stops of the discrete frames, film depends on that constant
stopping for its possiblity of reconstituting a moving reality—a reality which
is thus, in the very moment of appearance on screen, as the frames succeed

16. Giorgio de Chirico, *The Song of Love*. 1914. Oil on canvas, 28 ¾" × 23 ⅜";
Collection, The Museum of Modern Art, New York. Nelson A. Rockefeller
Bequest.

one another, perpetually flickered by the fading of its present presence, filled
with the *artifice* of its continuity and coherence."[23]

Through his foregrounding of still photography, Truffaut suggests that the
hidden desire of cinema all along has been immobility, as though images moved
only in search of the one, ideal image. To find that image, however, would be
to end all narrative—it would be the death of cinema. To put a memory into
words is to lose it, Calvino's Marco Polo tells the Emperor—therefore I will

17. The influence of de Chirico on Jean Cocteau's *Orphée* (Jean Marais as Orphée; Maria Casarès as the Princess).

18. The surrealist landscape of Jean Cocteau's *Orphée*: the Princess and Heurtebise go to their doom.

not speak of Venice. All his descriptions of cities tacitly assume Venice without naming it. The possibility of cinematic narrative depends on the not naming of Venice, on our *not* finding the one·image that will make all the others unnecessary.[24]

What is the ontological relation of narrative to death, and does this ontology shift somewhat when we speak of cinematic narrative? Peter Brooks in *Reading for the Plot* argues that the death wish was Freud's own masterplot for organic life, in the sense that the erotic and self-preservative drives are used in order to ward off the organism's inappropriate death; death, as Freud explains in *Beyond the Pleasure Principle*, is what makes our lives meaningful and subjects for narration.[25] Truffaut's Davenne also argues that his chapel needs the completion of only one more candle—his own. His life's meaning comes through the dead he has known; and his death will complete, in turn, the meaning of their lives. *La Chambre verte* shows the process of Davenne's constructing a death meant especially for him, in such as way that his end will be placed before his beginning, in the kind of effacement of origins that Brooks discerns in Freud's equation.[26]

Does the intertextual system of *La Chambre verte* reveal Truffaut to be a weak or a strong artist in relation to his precursor Cocteau? Certainly Truffaut's conflicting ways of dealing with his predecessor betray the "anxiety of influence" that Bloom talks about. Looking retrospectively over the oeuvre of Truffaut, this conflict between the joyful affirmation of the power of cinema on the one hand, and, on the other, the ascetic impulse to simplify and strip down artistic expression to the minimum, seems characteristic of most of Truffaut's films. The ascetic side is most often represented by characters who are writers or artists: Jules from *Jules et Jim* or the playwright Steiner in *The Last Metro*.

Despite the fact that Truffaut chooses to end *La Chambre verte* with the death of the artist, the power of cinema is never denied. Truffaut's other mentor, André Bazin, is very much present in this film as well. Bazin, in "The Myth of Total Cinema," wrote about the way cinema can arrest time, arguing that people recorded on film undergo a kind of "mummification" process—they are preserved in a timeless present. For Bazin, cinema was but the latest step in mankind's progress toward creating the perfect illusion of reality. "Total cinema" would be a form of representation in which the real would no longer appear as artifact. The apparatus would become invisible.[27]

Truffaut's testimonial to the power of his art is somewhat along these lines. On one point at least he corrects Cocteau and through that correction implicitly makes a stronger claim for the art of film than his predecessor. In Cocteau's film, Orphée, who has been ordered not to look upon Eurydice, is frightened when he sees a photograph of her—he is sure he is about to lose her forever. No, explains Heurtebise, a photograph is not the same as the person. When he does lose her, it is because he sees her in the rear-view mirror of a car. What for Cocteau was an ontological difference between mirror image and photographed image is dissolved for Truffaut. Cocteau's character Heurtebise explains to Orphée that one can see "death at work" in mirrors. His successor extends this to the photographic image.

Truffaut dramatizes the way in which a photograph may convey a greater sense of presence than the living person, if only because we are accustomed to perceive reality through conventions of representation. This could be the meaning of the title "la chambre verte" (the green chamber) which plays on the idea of "la chambre noire" or *camera obscura*. The photographic process, in our culture, is integral to our conception of life; thus it can be said to be green like a living plant. At the same time photographs and films make us conscious of the passing of time. While they are testimonials to life they are also proof of our own mortality. The mise-en-scène of Davenne's demise seems particularly self-referential when we consider that Truffaut, like Davenne, was said to be a great writer of obituaries. In *La Chambre verte* Truffaut has left us his own "testament of Orpheus," his own claim for the importance of his art and his defense of a life spent chasing down its fleeting shadows.

PART THREE

SUBJECTIVITY

In the previous chapter, I showed how François Truffaut struggled with the inheritance of his predecessor Cocteau, as he suffered and profited from the latter's influence. It is not by chance that the "anxiety of influence" is presented by Harold Bloom in exclusively masculine terms. The discourse of literature has, in the past at least, been an overwhelmingly masculine one. In film as well, the arranger is assumed to be male unless there are strongly marked indications to the contrary.

The tacit assumption that the source of a film story stems from a male enunciator exerts a subtle bias on cinematic narratives. Women characters are often portrayed as stages to be passed through, or as spaces to be invaded and conquered. The man's adventures become the dominant focus. Fortunately, however, this "patriarchal" slant in film narratives, even in films made by men, has not been monolithic.

Cinema was perceived by its first audiences as photography in motion. Projected publicly for the first time by the Lumière brothers in 1895 at the Grand Café in Paris, its fascination lay in realism. The audience is said to have jumped at the sight of the oncoming train in "L'Arrivée d'un train dans la gare de Ciotat" ("The Arrival of a train in the Ciotat station"). Apocryphal or not, the story underscores the point that the objective representation of motion, to the degree that a photograph of an object could be mistaken for the real thing, was the original impulse behind the creation of cinema.

But the end of the nineteenth century also marked a turn toward the subjective. The birth of cinema is contemporary with that of psychoanalysis. It wasn't long before filmmakers began to use film's apparent realism to portray fantasy and fiction. The Frenchman Georges Méliès staged a trip to the moon and to the North Pole. As early as 1906, Edwin S. Porter portrayed a world distorted by the subjective perception of a character. His "Dream of a Rarebit Fiend" portrays the perception and imagination of a man under the influence of alcohol.

Despite this promising beginning, the story of subjectivity has been one-sided in films. Although our culture traditionally considers men more "objective" and women more "subjective," the subjective thoughts of women characters are rarely emphasized in the films made by men. The camera almost never identifies with the point of view of the woman character, so that the spectators are also denied the option of identifying with her. Thus the technological apparatus of cinema itself often reinforces women's subordinate role in the narrative. The representation of women's subjectivity has had a complex history.

The first chapter of this section considers some exceptional instances in films made by men where the woman character participates in the telling of her own story. I describe how the literary technique of "dual narration" has been used in film to allow the fusion of the camera narrator with a woman character. Metadiegesis (the assumption of the storytelling function by a character in the story) is another way of marking a narrative as feminine. I analyze Alain Resnais's *Hiroshima mon amour* (written by Marguerite Duras) as one film which successfully presents the thoughts and feelings of the woman protagonist through metadiegesis. Unless the images and sound are presented consistently from the point of view of the woman character, however, the subjective quality is lost.

All of the strategies described may be used to open up points of resistance in the text to conventional storytelling. Of course, they they are not *necessarily* used that way; there is no intrinsically "progressive" film language.

Because film is a visual medium, space is an important area of cinematic expressiveness. This includes not only the two-dimensional "screen space" that gives a film its particular look, but also the three-dimensional "diegetic space." Diegetic space can be mediated through a character, through the point-of-view shot which is clearly attributable to the character's act of looking. As was the case with dual narration, the use of point-of-view shots lends importance to the character thus highlighted, whose perception becomes a link between the spectator and the story. The failure in film to mediate information about the diegetic space through women characters leads to the serious consequence of reinforcing a social fact of life: the cutting off of women from the full exploration of space. This not only reinforces cinematic stereotypes, but also conditions women as spectators and as actors in their real life roles.

In the second chapter, I deal with the relation between different types of film space and women protagonists. In a first section, I show how the relation between the woman character and the mise-en-scène of the film can become a metaphor for the character's state of mind. Ingmar Bergman and Woody Allen have both used these elements in their portrayal of the subjective thoughts and feelings of women protagonists. In their films, however, the women function principally as stand-ins for the director's male artistic persona. To some extent, they claim for themselves the capacity to embrace a feminine perspective. Against these models, Agnes Varda stands out as a director who employs some of the same techniques in order to explore what has historically been women's experience of space.

In some films, the woman character mentally resists the spaces that constrict her. By constructing a new relationship to space, she changes her self-image. In the end, I propose the new term "performative space" based on philospher J. L. Austin's concept of "performative utterances" in language. Women who take control of the spaces surrounding them, I suggest, both recreate themselves and influence the shape of the landscape that surrounds them. In turn, the films that represent this changed relation between a woman character and her surrounding space can be said to "perform" the possibility of a new construction of the self through language (in this instance, film language). Significantly, the two films that best exhibit this were made by literary authors: Peter Handke's *The Left-Handed Woman* and Marguerite Duras's *Nathalie Granger*.

The chapters in this section take their inspiration from feminist film criticism. Like some of the recent influential books in the field—Annette Kuhn's *Women's Pictures*, E. Ann Kaplan's *Women and the Cinema*, Teresa de Lauretis's *Alice Doesn't*, Mary Ann Doane's *The Desire to Desire*, and Lucy Fischer's *Shot/Countershot*—they attempt to develop a general view of women in the cinema that is based on the analysis of specific film texts.

CHAPTER
5

MEDIATED VISION
Women's Subjectivity

Rarely, in films made by men, do we get to know what the women characters are thinking and feeling. Having made that provocative statement, let me at once mention two exceptions. Kenji Mizoguchi's *The Life of Oharu* (*Saikaku ichidai onna*, 1952) portrays the unlucky existence of a well-born girl in seventeeth-century Japan, who in the course of a lifetime goes from court society to prostitution and begging (Figs. 19–21). In one of the pivotal shots of the film, Oharu has just been bought back by her parents from being a Shimabara courtesan. Stopping with her mother near a temple on the way home, she is drawn to the song of a beggar-woman who plays outside. Oharu, who has lived both at the Imperial Court and the palace of the Matsudaira Clan, recognizes the song as a court song, and learns that the beggar-woman shares a fate similar to her own—she also used to be a famous courtesan. In a beautifully framed shot, Mizoguchi shows Oharu reflecting on this coincidence. In the foreground, the beggar-woman sits with her back against a pillar of the temple. Slightly to the left of her, Oharu stands against the same pillar, which, with its companion off to screen left, also serves to frame her mother in the background.

In this one shot Mizoguchi sums up Oharu's life, past, present, and future; what is more, he shows us Oharu's realization of the meaning of her past and foreboding of the future. For Oharu *has been* a mother—she was sold to the Matsudaira Clan as a concubine in order to produce an heir—and like her own mother, she is cut off from her child. As it happens, this is to be the last time mother and daughter are together until they are both old women. And Oharu *will be* a beggar; it is as a beggar that she later gets the first glimpse of her child, now ten years old, who happens to stop in front of the temple where she is playing music. Mizoguchi's striking shot turns both forward and back, binding the film into a coherent statement about Oharu as individual and as type—as woman—whose fate is shared by others. But most importantly of all, in portraying Oharu's sympathy for the figure she will soon become, Mizoguchi encourages the spectator's identification with Oharu by using Oharu herself as surrogate for that spectator. In this shot, narrator and character speak as one.

Cut to Imperial Vienna, near the turn of the century. In *Letter from an Unknown Woman* (1958), Max Ophuls has created a mise-en-scène in which a man, on the eve of fighting a duel with the wronged husband of one of his mistresses, comes home to discover a letter from the woman in question. In reading the letter, he comes to see his whole life in a new light. Lisa outlines for him her childhood years, when she lived downstairs from him (Fig. 22), and two nights when he made love to her, once as a young woman, and later as a married woman. He had never recognized her as the same woman, and had never known the son she bore him. For Sebastian to read this letter, however, is to lose his life: reading it prevents him from getting away on time and thus avoiding the fatal duel with her husband (Fig. 23). Never has the compelling power of story-telling been more strongly stated! Lisa is a death-dealing Scheherazade who is in the position of telling her lover the unknown story of his own life. And, like Oharu, Lisa has been unable to speak out against the male world which has decreed her own lack of self-determination.

What is the story, from her point of view? Like Mizoguchi's, Ophuls's story turns on a pivotal shot in which character and narrator are fused into a compelling picture of past and future. As a young girl, Lisa was forced by her mother's remarriage to move to Graz, away from the Vienna flat which was just one floor away from Sebastian's. The impending departure brings to a crisis all her unavowed feelings for him, so she escapes from the train station where her mother and stepfather are waiting and runs back to hide on the stairs just above his flat and await his return. But when he does return, it is in the company of another woman. From her position on the stairway, she is the agonized witness of his progress up the winding staircase with the woman who blocks her from breaking her silence. As spectators, we know that she wishes herself in that woman's place.

When she reaches a marriageable age, Lisa returns to Vienna and posts herself outside the building Sebastian occupies until he finally notices her. She is careful not to tell him too much about herself, and she knows him well enough to hope that he will call up the usual script and take *her* home this time. This is in fact what happens; Sebastian calls off his rehearsal and his rendezvous with another woman to escort his new conquest first to dinner, then to a fair-grounds (Fig. 24) and dance hall, and finally to his flat. As Lisa and Sebastian ascend the stairs, the camera watches from the very position where young Lisa stood in agony a few years before. Again, the perspective of the third-person camera narrator and the character are fused as the spectator realizes that Lisa's alter ego also watches from that position, triumphing in her success. Yet, although able on the one hand to identify with Lisa's happiness, the spectator also identifies with the third-person narrator and knows that she is no different from the others, as far as Sebastian is concerned.[1] In a future moment, Lisa will again ascend the staircase to find herself betrayed by herself, as Sebastian

19. Oharu as concubine to the head of the Matsudaira clan (Kinuyo Tanaka). (Kenji Mizoguchi, *The Life of Oharu*)

20. Oharu being courted by her future husband. (Kenji Mizoguchi, *The Life of Oharu*)

21. Oharu as a prostitute. (Kenji Mizoguchi, *The Life of Oharu*)

22. Lisa as a young girl fascinated by Sebastian Brandt (Joan Fontaine and Louis Jourdan). (Max Ophuls, *Letter from an Unknown Woman*)

23. The captive reader: Sebastian with Lisa's letter (Louis Jourdan). (Max Ophuls, *Letter from an Unknown Woman*)

24. Lisa and Sebastian at the fairgrounds. (Max Ophuls, *Letter from an Unknown Woman*)

tries to seduce her without recognizing her as the woman he has known before (yet ironically, each time he meets her he uses the same line: "I feel I've seen you somewhere before").

Two moments in two films, both depending on repetition to give us the feeling of being simultaneously inside and outside a character; on the one hand this repetition links us with her past, showing the present through her eyes, the eyes of one already experienced with the world; on the other hand it looks toward her future, so that we know more than she does about the pattern being insidiously woven around her.

The two shots described above are instances of the "dual narrative mode" in which the authority of the film narrator is for a moment suspended; the narrator *says* what the character *means*.[2] This is one technique film directors have at their disposal to let us know what a character thinks and feels.[3]

DUAL NARRATION

Like literary narratives, film fictions are *told*. Because the overall story of a film includes sounds, music, and dialogue as well as images, I have said that it is convenient to think of the storyteller as an "arranger," that is as the agency responsible for the final arrangement of all these elements into the whole. On both the image and sound tracks, the arranger is responsible for what is seen and heard and how the images and sounds are put together.[4]

Having said this, I should note that the similarity between literary and film narratives, particularly in the area of the portrayal of a character's subjective thoughts and feelings, is in some dispute. In *Novels into Film*, George Bluestone comments: "With the abandonment of language as its sole and primary element, the film necessarily leaves behind those characteristic contents of thought which only language can approximate, tropes, dreams, memories, conceptual consciousness."[5] Christian Metz has asserted that the cinema "lags behind verbal language in portraying interiority, dislocations in point of view, temporal ellipses, the capacity to abstract, metaphor, the range of more or less figurative meanings, etc., and finally in the ability to analyze proper."[6]

The problem, as Siegfried Kracauer notes, is to find physical correspondences for the mental continuum.[7] The peculiarity of film language is that our understanding arises out of our perception of sounds and images. The editing may guide this understanding to some degree; but the selection of sounds and images by the arranger does so also. A fiction film does not denote except by connotation, because it presents a "pseudo-world" especially created to produce an effect on the spectator. There are no fixed meanings to the images and sounds of a film; they are organized for the spectator according to strategies of coherence.

One of those strategies is that of controlling point of view. As the French novelist Alain Robbe-Grillet astutely noted, the film shot always implies a point of view: it must always be taken *from* somewhere.[8] This means that, in addition to the arranger, we must posit a narrator whose point of view, in most instances, is revealed by the camera.

In film, the narrator-presence is revealed by the point of view from which the story is being presented at any one moment of the narrative. Some literary parameters apply also to film. For instance, Tzvetan Todorov has pointed out that the literary narrator knows either more, less, or as much as his or her character(s). Todorov calls these three positions unfocalized, externally focalized, and internally focalized, respectively.[9] The film narrator can assume any of these three positions. In the dual mode, the narrator temporarily suspends omniscience in order to limit itself to the character's thoughts, perceptions, or feelings, while at the same time maintaining an ironic distance from the character; while saying more than the character *knows*, the narrator implies what the character *thinks*, thus partially identifying with the point of view of the character.

The dual narrative mode is an important means of encouraging the spectator's identification with the character, since the tendency of point-of-view shots to determine our sympathy and identification is so strong that it is almost impossible to resist on intellectual grounds. To cite a recent example, in Wolfgang Peterson's *Das Boot* (1982), we identify with the Germans who are trying to slip through the English defenses at Gibraltar because the camera espouses the point of view of the Germans inside the ship; the spectator is made to feel his or her way into the space of the German submarine. Thus our sympathies are all on the German side while watching the film, even if objectively we don't wish that Germany had won World War II.

An example from a literary work may serve to clarify how instances of dual narration can be identified. In the following passage from Malcolm Lowry's *Under the Volcano*, I have italicized the passage presented in the dual mode (in order to avoid confusion, the term "amour propre" in the second sentence is set in Roman type rather than the author's italics):

> By the time he reached the Palace the sun had set. In spite of his amour propre he immediately regretted having come. *The broken pink pillars, in the half-light, might have been waiting to fall down on him: the pool, covered with green scum, its steps torn away and hanging by one rotting clamp, to close over his head. The shattered evil-smelling chapel, overgrown with weeds, the crumbling walls, splashed with urine, on which scorpions lurked— wrecked entablature, sad archivolt, slippery stones covered with excreta— this place, where love had once brooded, seemed part of a nightmare.* And Laruelle was tired of nightmares.[10]

In literature, the first-person can be substituted for the third-person pronoun in a passage written in the dual mode without any loss of coherence. In order for the dual situation to be perceived in cinema, a film must first set up a norm and then depart from it in a way that makes it clear the departure is occasioned by the perceptual or emotional input of the character. Hollywood films as well as "art cinema" films have used this technique in order to portray the feelings of their characters.

In classical Hollywood narrative, the spatial cues are carefully delineated so that the spectator is never disoriented. The narrator is effaced in the sense that the spectator is invited to imagine him or herself into the diegetic space and to forget that the story is actually happening on a two-dimensional screen and being presented from a limited point of view.[11] The dual narrative situation is relatively rare because it breaks with the third-person, omniscient narration that is characteristic of this style. Hitchcock is one director who uses the technique occasionally to heighten the spectator's identification with a character in a dangerous situation. In a sequence of *North by Northwest* (1959), for instance, Hitchcock moves his camera slightly to the left of the cornfield where Cary Grant is hiding from the attack plane, and somewhat closer to the ground than in the previous shots. Even though the shot in question is not strictly from Grant's point of view (the shot is not from within the cornfield), the low angle shows us how he feels about the attack because the plane, from this angle, bears down menacingly. Because of this shot we identify with Grant rather than with the pilot, whose thoughts and feelings are not conveyed to us.

An understanding of how the dual narrative mode functions can simplify some apparently complicated moments in classical cinema. In a well-known article about *Stagecoach* (1939), Nick Browne focuses on the scene in which Dallas, the prostitute who has been run out of town, finds herself uncomfortably at table with Lucy, a respectable married woman. Browne argues that all the shots in the sequence can either be attributed to Lucy's point of view ("series A") or to an objective respresentation of Lucy's social dominance and formal privilege ("series B"). Yet he notes that while Lucy is established as the center of spatial legibility in the sequence, the spectator, surprisingly, identifies with Dallas rather than Lucy. Accounting for this forces Browne to postulate a divided consciousness in the spectator ("evidently, a spectator is several places at once—with the fictional viewer, with the viewed, and at the same time in a position to evaluate and respond to the claims of each").[12]

Matters can be greatly simplified by reading the "series B" shots as instances of dual narration that represents a fusion of Dallas's sensibility with that of the narrator. The identification of the viewer with the narrating voice is thereby maintained. The shots of "series B" that are taken from a position that Dallas could not literally occupy function in the same way as similar shots in *North by Northwest*; they show how the Dallas character *feels* about Lucy's disdain for her. Positing the dual narrative mode removes the necessity for Browne's questionable claim that in this sequence we manage to identify with the characters rather than with the point of view of the camera.

The dual narrative mode is frequent in European art-cinema narration. Here the conditions are ideal because of the presence of a strongly defined camera narrator. Directors such as Alain Resnais, Michelangelo Antonioni, and François Truffaut, for example, eschew the self-effacement of the classical Hollywood style. At the same time, art cinema films place an emphasis on character and individual experience.[13] With both halves of the dual narrative situation so clearly marked, the technique is relatively easy to achieve. Buñuel uses it in *Tristana* to strengthen our identification with the heroine, by allowing us to supply a subjective thought which is not spelled out in the narration.

Tristana is divided into four parts, each of which is separated in diegetic time by a period of two years. From one part to the next, the relationship between the narrator and the main character changes. Overall, the movement is from unfocalized (part one) to internally focalized (part two) to externally focalized (parts three and four) and back to internally focalized narration (end of part four). Dual narration is strongest in part two and at the end of part four.

The narrator's self-dramatization makes it possible to identify the dual narrative situations that occur later. The opening shot of Toledo shows the bell-tower of a church in the background, prefiguring a dream that the heroine has later. Tristana (Catherine Deneuve) and her maid Saturna are shown walking toward the camera; at the end of the film they will walk away from the camera in a continuation of the same sequence. Thus the narrator announces its presence by framing the story within a single sequence. The narrator's presence is also foregrounded in the way that the principal male character is introduced. Don Lope (played by Fernando Rey) is mentioned in a conversation on the playing field, whereupon the camera cuts to a brief scene where he is discovered flirting with a young woman.

Throughout the first part of the film, Tristana is kept at a distance. At the same time, one-half of the scenes end with the focus on the heroine. For instance, when she has a nightmare, Don Lope comes in to see what is the

25. Tristana's visit to the belltower (Catherine Deneuve). (Luis Buñuel, *Tristana*)

matter. As he leaves, the camera remains with Tristana who watches him walk away. A visit to the bell tower focuses on Tristana's look as she ascends the stairs (Fig. 25). A dinner scene where she inexplicably cries while Don Lope and Saturna talk about her ends with the camera focused on her; even the sequence of Don Lope talking to his male friends in the café ends with a shot of Tristana. By the end of part one, she has become the focal character of the film. Yet the narrator still retains its superiority and distance—it knows more than she does. This is shown in the very scene which would appear most subjective: the heroine's dream, in which Don Lope's head appears swinging in the bell of the belltower just mentioned. The dream prefigures her ultimate revolt against this relative who turns her into his mistress. At this stage the heroine does not yet understand the meaning of her own unconscious thoughts.

It is in part two that a type of dual narration occurs, bringing the spectator closer to the heroine's thoughts and feelings. In one such sequence, Tristana is at a table in front of a plate of chickpeas. The script reads: "She picks up two of them and places them on the tablecloth. She looks from one to the other.

26. Nana (Anna Karina) with Raoul (Saddy Rebot). (Jean-Luc Godard, *Vivre sa vie*)

We are made to understand tht she is trying to choose between them. Closeup shot of the two chickpeas. The hand of Tristana hesitates over one and then the other chickpea. In the end she takes one of them. Forward tracking shot toward Tristana. She chews it slowly with a certain satisfaction."[14] The possibility of conveying thought with this sequence has been prepared previously when Tristana says that she often amuses herself in trying to choose between things which look alike. This apparently insignificant subjective moment prepares us for Tristana's later hesitation at calling the doctor after her uncle's heart attack. She decides not to and he dies.

Jean-Luc Godard used the dual narative mode in *Vivre sa vie* in order to facilitate the viewer's identification with his character Nana (Fig. 26). At one point Nana sits in a café writing a job application to a house of prostitution. The camera records in closeup the forming of each letter, intercut with one shot in which she sits thinking, and another where she stands up and measures herself. The dual situation arises from the intimate, closed space created by the subjective view of the letter she is writing; the spectator is literally "looking over her shoulder." That space is suddenly invaded by Raoul's hand, who covers the writing (Figs. 27–28). In the rest of the film, he will literally "blot her out." What we have seen is her last moment of privacy.

The fact that dual narration plays such an important role in identification gives a clue as to why it so seldom occurs with women characters: for films seldom allow the spectator any depth of identification with a woman. Instead, the female star is most often offered to the spectator as an object to be looked at—her makeup, the lighting used to enhance her features, and even her traditionally passive role in the plot contribute to making her an object for visual consumption. This way of presenting women is a tradition of Western art and presupposes a male spectator.[15] Films that conform to this tradition tacitly put into place both an arranger and a third-person camera narrator that the spectator assumes to be male. As I will show in the next chapter, some filmmakers have managed to make films that assume a female arranger. Consequently, I will use "he" or "she" when speaking of this narrating agency. For the camera-narrator, I prefer the impersonal "it" proposed by Mieke Bal.[16]

As the point and focus for the voyeuristic spectacle of cinema, the male spectator identifies with the cinematic apparatus that subjects the woman to its ideological deformation, thus reaffirming man's traditional exercise of power over women, who become the bearers of his look. For the woman spectator, the glamorized presentation of the female star may release a desire to be the star, to take the place of the screen presence that receives the homage of the male viewer as well as that of the male characters in the story. As in the case of the male viewer, this process reflects a social reality: "*Men act* and *women appear*. Men look at women. Women watch themselves being looked at. This determines not only most relations between men and women but also the relation of women to themselves. The surveyor of woman in herself is male: the surveyed female. Thus she turns herself into an object—and most particularly an object of vision—a sight."[17]

In addition to the visual presentation of the character on film (something we might call the "screen character"), one can also speak of his or her actions in the narration; to this end, we might speak of the "diegetic character." It is this diegetic character who may become the focus for dual narration. Because the "diegetic character" of the male star is more rounded, the man who identifies with his male counterpart will find his active, dominant role in society reinforced. If he mimics the star later in his daily life, it will make it easier for him to play the role traditionally assigned to him by society. By contrast, the "diegetic character" of the woman is often seriously underdeveloped: she is defined by what men think of her and how they treat her, the camera rarely espouses her point of view, and the narrator almost never shares the responsibility for telling the story with her in the dual narrative situation. A woman who identifies with and mimics a female star condemns herself to portraying a flat "screen character"—a visual spectacle without an active role. For this reason, the dual narrative mode, which does develop women as rounded "diegetic characters," is an important device.

27. Nana writing her letter. (Jean-Luc Godard, *Vivre sa vie*)

28. Raoul interrupts Nana's letter. (Jean-Luc Godard, *Vivre sa vie*)

METADIEGESIS

Occasionally in film the story (or part of it) will be told by a woman character. Here, if anywhere, we might expect to see the world through a woman's eyes. But in practice it is very hard to mark a narrative so that it remains subjective; careful reading usually reveals that in these so-called metadiegetic narratives many of the camera shots show things that the narrating character couldn't have seen or couldn't have perceived from that angle. Hitchcock plays on this in *Stage Fright* (1950), where he counts on the spectator's forgetting that the initial story of the murder is in fact an alibi narrative, told (as it turns out) by the murderer himself.[18] *Letter from an Unknown Woman* and *The Life of Oharu* are both stories that are marked at the outset as being told by women (through a letter and memories respectively), yet the subjective view is not maintained in the course of the film; indeed, this is what makes the use of the *dual* narrative mode possible.

The lack of film narratives that are clearly marked as stories told by women is striking, given the abundance, in mainstream twentieth century literature, of inner landscapes of the feminine psyche. I am thinking in particular of Faulkner's (*The Sound and the Fury*), Joyce's (*Ulysses*), and Woolf's (*Mrs. Dalloway*). In film one of the few equivalent examples is Resnais's and Duras's *Hiroshima mon amour*.

Although the story in this film is not told consistently from the woman character's point of view, significant metadiegetic portions are anchored in the woman character as narrator. *Hiroshima mon amour* portrays the love affair in Hiroshima between Riva, a French actress, and Okada, a Japanese architect. She has come to Hiroshima fourteen years after the war (the bomb) to act in a film on peace; she meets him the day before her departure, and in the few hours remaining to them they reach an understanding of themselves and of their historical past, both personal and national. One of Resnais's recurrent themes is that history must be lived subjectively to be felt and remembered: Okada can thus reproach Riva with "You saw nothing at Hiroshima" even though she has visited the museums, the hospitals, and the war memorials. In this film, seeing becomes a metaphor for understanding; the status of the film image thereby becomes foregrounded, actively challenging the interpretive capacities of the film spectator.

The process of reaching understanding—of seeing—begins as Riva, who has gotten up and stands on the terrace of her hotel room, looks back at Okada lying on the bed. Abruptly the point-of-view shifts to a shot of Okada's arm, followed by a subjective shot of the arm of Riva's German lover of fourteen years before as he lay dying in a pool of blood. This lapse into metadiegetic narration lasts only for a brief moment—a moment that, however, initiates the double temporal strand of the film that will begin to unwind under the pressing questions of Okada.

For Riva, past and present come together in the bar where Okada stimulates her memory with alcohol and leading questions. As Riva delves deeper and deeper into her past all diegetic (realistic) sound from the bar is excluded, except for the sound of their voices. The soundtrack itself is presented from the point of view of Riva, whose concentration on her story blots out all surrounding noise. Gradually the voices of Riva and Okada become a voice-over for images from Riva's past affair with the German soldier, presented first in flashes and then with increasing clarity. These images are clearly from her point of view, yet the sound of her narrating voice, and of Okada's prompting, remains anchored in the present; the intrusion of sound from the past is limited to a single scream as she recounts coming home after being shorn of her hair by the village authorities. On the other hand the absence of other realistic sound from the bar where Riva sits telling her story and the fact that she addresses Okada as though he were her dead German lover ("I loved blood ever since I had tasted yours") clearly establish Riva as the narrator. The third-person narrator takes over the story again at the point when Okada slaps her to wake her up from her immersion in the past. At this point the realistic sound from the bar returns. This recovery of sound perfectly corresponds to her own description of her recovery from madness during the war: "At six o'clock in the evening, the cathedral of St. Etienne rings, in summer as in winter. One day, it is true, I can hear it . . . I start to see again. I remember having been able to see before—while we were lovers, while we were happy." This parallelism implicitly suggests that her telling the story to Okada is a kind of cure.

Later, in her hotel room, Riva reproaches herself for having debased her love with the German soldier by putting it into narrative form. Riva looks at her reflection in the mirror; although her lips do not move, her voice accuses her in a metadiegetic voice-over: "I told our story. You see, it could be told." Metadiegetic sound continues as she walks through the street, with Okada following a certain distance behind while the camera cuts between traveling shots down the streets of Hiroshima to traveling shots down the streets of Nevers. In a cadenced voice-over that anchors this cross-cutting to her internal thoughts, she makes the parallel between love and death that the two cities, Nevers and Hiroshima, have come to signify for her: "I was waiting for you calmly, with boundless impatience. Devour me. Deform me to your image so that no one else, after you, will understand at all the reason for so much desire. A time will come. In which we will no longer be capable of naming that which will unite us. The name will be effaced from our memory. And then, it will disappear altogether."

By focusing on a woman protagonist, *Hiroshima mon amour* contributes much to our identification with the historical experience of women. We gain a greater understanding of what it means to be passive, in love as in war, to be the one who *waits*. Resnais has achieved this in part by a narrative structure that skillfully represents the heroine's subjective experience of time. The French critic Marie-Claire Ropars has argued that this portrayal of "lived time" (*temps vécu*) brings cinema closer to the novel: "By observing the different ways in which people pass through time, we become witnesses to the different ways that time passes over them."[19] But Riva's transgression is also a transgression of space. In Nevers, Riva's appropriation of the space in which she meets her German lover is finally punished by the authorities for whom such freedom is a transgression. In Hiroshima, the streets become another labyrinth that echoes the imprisoning streets of Nevers. In the next chapter, some of the implications of that spatial transgression will be discussed in more detail.

CHAPTER

6

WOMEN AND FILM SPACE

In the preceding chapter I gave two exceptional examples in which the task of telling the story is shared by a film narrator and a woman character, allowing the spectator access into the character's subjectivity—her thoughts, feelings, and perceptions. In this chapter I want to focus on one aspect of film narrative— that of space—in order to show how this, too, can become the means of expressing subjectivity.

The French feminist critic Claudine Hermann has pointed out that "space, for the woman, is by definition a place of frustration, whether physical, moral, or cultural. It is also the place of systematization and hierarchization."[1] Nowhere, perhaps, does the subordination of women appear more clearly than in their treatment in cinematic space.

There is, first of all, the two-dimensional screen space, in which women are glamorized, handed over to the spectator as objects to be looked at. The star may be visually enhanced through mise-en-scène (make-up, lighting, and the placing of the character in exotic and ornamental settings) and montage (for instance, through use of the close-up).

Secondly, women are conventionally positioned in the three-dimensional, diegetic space in a manner that makes them seem more passive than the male characters. In the first place, most point-of-view shots are authorized by the look of male characters. Secondly, women characters are less likely to initiate action. This means that they function like two-dimensional figures, similar to the landscapes against which they are photographed.

Some films have partially overcome this limiting portrayal of women. A first group uses mise-en-scène as a metaphor for the woman character's state of mind. Agnes Varda uses this technique very effectively in showing the psychological constriction of her heroine in Sans toit ni loi (Vagabond), made in 1985. When it is employed by male directors such as Woody Allen and Ingmar Bergman, however, the woman often comes to stand for their own artistic personae. We can therefore wonder how much these films really portray about the subjectivity of their women characters. Instead, the man's choice of a woman protagonist may only reflect the traditional view that objectivity is masculine, and subjectivity feminine.

In the section on identification, I suggest that the use of point-of-view shots that are authorized by the look of a woman character do help the spectator to identify with her. The spectator whose information about the diegetic space is given through a woman character's eyes perceives that character as much more developed.

Finally, I explore the idea that the diegetic space can become the site of a resistance on the part of the women characters. In the two films discussed in the final section, the rebelling women identify with their domestic space and use it to create a place for themselves outside of patriarchal domination.

MISE-EN-SCÈNE AS METAPHOR

In some films the world presented by the arranger is colored by the mind of a character, so that the whole film or significant portions of it can be read as the equivalent of a state of mind. When the character is a woman, the film often manages to say something important about what has historically been women's experience. Here, for once, the arranger seems female rather than male.

Agnes Varda uses the technique in *Sans toit ni loi*. Even though the narrative takes the form of interviews with those who have known the heroine Mona, the wintery landscape and the camera's insistence on filming signs of decay—the peeling paint of a garage or badly maintained chateau, rotting plane trees, barren vineyards, abandoned buildings and people wearing rags—add up to a statement about the inner vacuousness of the main character. However, they legitimize her aimless wandering by showing that the people who perceive her as marginal are in fact as infected as she is. She has owned up to the fact; they haven't.

The narration itself is decentered in space, as the anchor of the interviews in realistic diegetic time or space is purposefully called into question. Many of the interviews do not presuppose a listening Other, but seem like voiced thoughts. We are never shown anyone actually interviewing the characters. One of Mona's lovers speaks from the platform of a freight train as it pulls away, while another friend, Yolande, addresses the camera directly without any prompting on the part of an interviewer. A woman who gives Mona water expresses a wish to be free, like Mona—again, she seems to be talking to herself. Others are blocked by a physical separation from any interviewer—the garage owner speaks from behind a glass pane. One couple, a foreman and his wife, is merely overheard discussing Mona while watching television.

Through the lack of point-of-view shots Varda has distanced herself from the norms of art cinema narration in order to underscore a philosophical point.

On the other hand Varda uses some of those norms for her own ends. Throughout the film, the camera-narrator seems to have its own agenda, following a little girl dressed in red down the street after Mona has already entered the bakery, and otherwise "indulging" in the exploration of pictorial space.

The color red becomes a kind of theme. A red scarf is abandoned on the sacks of grain; a woman comes out of the shower draped in a red towel. Rhyming shots are used to open and close the film. In the film's opening shot, two poplar trees standing near the ditch where Mona dies are prominently featured; when her ride lets her off near the same trees toward the end, we know that the moment of narrative closure is coming. Varda also repeats the mirror shots and shots through glass which already marked her style in *Cleo de 5 à 7* (*Cleo from 5 to 7*, 1962). The end result of Varda's filmmaking style is to force us to identify Mona's state of mind with the bleak landscape she traverses, while her alienation is underscored by the remoteness and distance of the interviewees from the narrator.

In films made by men, the strategy of presenting the world as an extension of a female personality is often used as a metaphor for the filmmaker's artistic persona. Ingmar Bergman and Woody Allen both exemplify this practice; in *Persona* and *Interiors* they are simultaneously exploring some of the problems of the artistic mind through female characters and making statements about femininity. In both films, however, women are shown in very traditional terms.

In *Interiors* (1978), Woody Allen manages to express the mother's psychotic depression in the pale pastels and whites of her interior decorating, while her daughter Renata's anxiety neurosis is mirrored in the outside world. As Renata (Diane Keaton) goes through the crisis of not being able to write her poem, the camera cuts to the gnarled and tangled branches of a barren, wintery tree outside. Later on in the film, a shot of Renata staring at the ocean is followed by a shot in which the ocean waves comes forward toward her in a threatening way. If we identify with Renata, we are bound to feel an overwhelming sensation of anxiety at this point. If, in addition, we recall the recurrent theme of the artist's anxiety in Allen's other films, this scene reads as a portrayal of his own artistic problems.

In the wintery scene where Renata and Joey walk together with their mother, Renata's lack of an empathic connection with her sister is echoed in the lack of color which repeats in nature the type of interior their mother has continually subjected them to. In contrast, the woman their father wants to marry wears a red dress which the daughters find loud and vulgar.

The remoteness between the characters also finds expression in the framing of the camera. In the opening sequence of the film, the camera shows three shots of the mother's "interior," her empty beach house. In the fourth shot, Joey appears in a mirror. Three more shots frame her progress through the first floor and her ascent up the stairs until she comes to rest on screen right in a medium close-up next to a window. A point-of-view shot shows three little girls playing on the beach below—a scene from the girls' childhood. The camera returns to Joey, still at screen right, then cuts to Renata on screen left, with her hand against the window, as though she is trying to touch or reach something through it. The sisters' psychological isolation from one another is conveyed by their separation on opposite sides of the screen in these two successive shots. The next shot is a rear shot of the father who begins to speak about his marriage

29. Woody Allen's intertext: *Persona.* (Ingmar Bergman, *Persona*)

with Eve. Again, psychological distance is indicated by the shift in diegetic space: the father speaks against the background of city skyscrapers. This introductory section concludes with a restatement of each character's physical and mental isolation: a shot of the three little girls on the beach, the shot of Joey on screen right, the shot of Renata on screen left, the father with his back to the camera.

When Renata raises her hand against the glass in the opening scene, Woody Allen is quoting a similar shot in the prologue sequence of Ingmar Bergman's *Persona* (1967), when the young boy rubs his palm against an opaque glass screen on which the images of Alma and Elizabeth alternately come in and out of focus (Fig. 29). Although ostensibly focusing on female characters, Bergman, like Allen, constructs a compelling psychological portrait of the artist. At one moment in the film, his character Elizabeth turns to look at the spectator and points her camera at us (Fig. 30). The women in these films become to some extent the vehicles for the expression of the (male) director's problems. It is as though the director identified his persona as artist with a feminine side of himself, a conception of the artist that Freud seems to have shared.

In *Persona*, the actress Elizabeth's refusal to speak, which necessitates her departure for a rest cure on the coast in the company of her nurse Alma, stands for Bergman's sense of the futility of film language. Viewed in this perspective, the opening prologue with its series of disjointed images (many of them from

30. Elizabeth (Liv Ullmann) photographing the film spectator. (Ingmar Bergman, *Persona*)

31. The mirror shot in Alma's (Bibi Anderson) imaginary or dream sequence. (Ingmar Bergman, *Persona*)

Bergman's earlier films) reads as a visual "writer's block." The trajectory of the film is a voyage through the apparatus of cinema, which is consistently thematized. At the end of the film, it is not just Elizabeth but film language itself that begins to "speak" again.[2]

In the film's greatest moment of crisis, the two strands of the narrative coalesce as Alma sets a piece of glass in the path where Elizabeth is sure to step on it with her bare feet. Her cruelty is motivated by her reading of Elizabeth's letter to the doctor, in which she expresses her ironic distance toward Alma. At the moment when Elizabeth steps on the glass, her reaction of pain is supplemented by a shot of celluloid film burning. Bergman's script states that the spectator should feel the film has broken. In the overall metalinguistic allegory of the film, it is possible to read Alma's cutting of Elizabeth as a statement that language must assault its audience to remain alive. The French surrealist Antonin Artaud had expressed a similar idea in his writings, where he argued that theater should use a language of objects that translates mental anguish into real, physical pain. In the "First Manifesto on the Theater of Cruelty," first published in 1932, he writes that "The theater will never find itself again . . . except by furnishing the spectator with the truthful precipitates of dreams, in which his taste for crime, his erotic obsessions, his savagery, his chimeras, his utopian sense of life and matter, even his cannibalism, pour out, on a level not counterfeit and illusory, but interior."[3] Alma's repeated acts of violence, physical and verbal, against Elizabeth are exteriorizations of her patient's own violent feelings. By giving them physical expression, she paves the way for Elizabeth's reintegration into reality. Bergman makes this into a statement about his relationship to film art as well.

As part of his critical examination of the cinematic apparatus, Bergman questions the mechanisms of identification. Alma is the spectator's stand-in, a member of the audience who suddenly finds herself in the privileged position of talking back to the actress. (Alma says to Elizabeth: "I saw you in your last film. I thought I could become you—inside.") This statement prepares the spectator for a series of images in which Alma and Elizabeth become interchangeable.

In the first of these, Elizabeth gets up during the night and walks through Alma's room. A shot in which she is shown framed in the doorway is followed by one in which she looks out with Alma toward the spectator, or at a mirror that is not shown in the diegetic space. Wordlessly, Elizabeth draws Alma's hair away from her forehead, similar to the way she wears her own. The film spectator is made to feel that Elizabeth is suggesting a physical resemblance between herself and Alma. Both women stand looking at the "mirror," which occupies the position of the film spectator. In the morning, Elizabeth denies having come to see Alma during the night, so that we don't know whether the scene was a fantasy or a dream of Alma's. The "mirror" in the shot, which enables the spectator to look at the women looking at themselves (Fig. 31), intensifies the impression that Alma seeing herself as Elizabeth is a surrogate for the spectator's identification with Alma and Elizabeth. After the resolution of Elizabeth's crisis, this "mirror" shot reappears: as Alma prepares to leave the cottage, she reimagines that scene while looking in a mirror that, this time, is represented in the diegetic space. With her right hand, Alma pulls back her hair from her forehead; Elizabeth's remembered gesture is then superimposed on the mirror image.

In a second dream or fantasy scene, Elizabeth's face looms in the foreground while Alma plays Elizabeth to the actress's husband (Fig. 32). Elizabeth is put in the position of "learning her lines" again from an understudy. Finally, the two women's faces are merged as Alma recites in a voice-over Elizabeth's difficulty in imagining herself as a mother (Fig. 33). It is obvious that in using motherhood as a mythological expression of womanhood, Bergman equates the feminine with nature.[4]

Through her identification with Elizabeth, Alma is able to exteriorize her patient's inner state. The remarkable resolution of the crisis comes as Alma recites disconnected words, then tears at her own flesh so Elizabeth can drink her blood, a scene that once again recalls Artaud's "theater of cruelty."

The spectator in *Persona* actually passes through the projector and comes out on the other side; the first shot in the opening sequence shows an arc lamp connecting to begin the film projection, and the final shot is that of the lamp disconnecting again. As in Fellini's *8 ½*, the film being discussed in *Persona* is the very film we are seeing. The metafilmic dimension of *Persona* seems, in the end, more successful than Bergman's attempt at portraying a woman's state of mind. Like Woody Allen, he has managed to tell us a lot about himself as an artist but very little about women.[5]

IDENTIFICATION

In the previous chapter, I described the way in which the dual narrative mode can strengthen our identification with a character. The spectator will almost always identify with the character whose look authorizes a point-of-view shot. At the same time, as David Bordwell and Kristin Thompson point out, it is important to distinguish *depth* of identification; most point-of-view shots denote only perceptual subjectivity, not mental subjectivity.[6] Edward Branigan distinguishes between projective point-of-view shots (which refer to a specific mental state of the character) and reflective shots (which reveal only the presence or normal awareness of the character).[7] The dual narrative mode is built upon projective point-of-view shots, and encourages a stronger identification because we actually enter into the thoughts and feelings of the character. Yet even the reflective point-of-view shot can further our sense of identification because the character's view of the diegetic space becomes the means of our own introduction to it. This is true even though a reflective shot may not be marked as subjective at all, but be part of the code of a given narrative style; an example is the shot-counter-shot used in filming conversation in classical narrative.

For example, Claudia Weill's *Girlfriends* centers on the ambitions of a young

32. Alma plays Elizabeth to the actress's husband. (Ingmar Bergman, *Persona*)

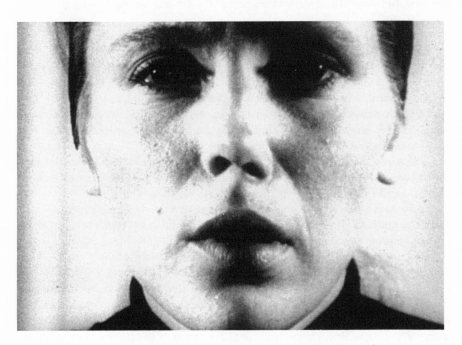

33. The merging of identities. (Ingmar Bergman, *Persona*)

woman photographer in New York, Sue Weinblatt.[8] She has been trying to sell work for some time with little success. The key to a breakthrough is important contacts, and since she is not yet known she has none of these. This fact is dramatized for her and for us in a pivotal scene where she enters the "O. K. Harris Agency." In the establishing shot for the scene, Sue comes down the corridor toward a woman who blocks the camera's view in the foreground, just as she will try to block Sue's access to the art agent, Mr. Karpel. This first shot is mediated not by Sue, but by an intrusive narrator who metaphorically closes off the diegetic space, giving the visual equivalent of the rejection Sue can expect. The next shots cut back and forth between Sue and the assistant, as we watch the woman simultaneously ignore her (she continues to work on her slides) and block her from taking another step in the direction of her future ("Mr. Karpel never sees anyone without an appointment"; "The secretary's not here now to make an appointment"; "come back after lunch"; etc.). Because the camera has followed Sue from outside the agency, the viewer identifies with her desire to succeed in penetrating into Karpel's office, to break out of the spatial confinement that threatens to stifle her career. There *is* no future for her unless she can reach the space of Mr. Karpel's office.

The camera now resumes a position behind the head of the assistant. Sue turns to go back down the corridor, but thinks better of it. Turning back toward the camera, she decides to claim (falsely) that she was sent by a famous person, recogizable to Karpel and the assistant. Her announcement is followed by a cut back to the assistant from Sue's point of view, motioning her to go in.

The space Sue now enters is male-dominated and she is subjugated once more. She appears as a suppliant figure off to screen left while Karpel sits behind a huge desk. In the foreground, pictures leaning against the desk push him even further into remoteness. An enormous print of a nude female torso hangs behind his head. He is a modern version of the Wizard of Oz, surrounded by the apparatus of his trade. Karpel looks at Sue's pictures—ironically, the closest look we ever have of them is from *his* point of view. Yet before she leaves, Sue is on the way back from alienation, because Karpel has found her a "fairy godmother" who will exhibit her work.

Girlfriends shows the value in having diegetic space explored by the mediating agency of a female protagonist; even perceptual point-of-view shots lend importance to the goals of female characters, creating what Lucy Fischer has called "positive identification."[9] Yet for the most part, film narratives are told from the point of view of the camera narrator while male characters get most of the point-of-view shots.

Even more rarely are women allowed projective point-of-view shots which allow the spectator to guess at their mental states. This is true even when the man and woman are equally important to the story. An example is François Truffaut's *The Woman Next Door* (1981), which depicts the passionate and doomed love affair between two neighbors who are thrown together by chance after having separated violently some years before. On only two occasions do we see Mathilde Bauchard (Fanny Ardant) looking out the window at Bernard

Coudray (Gérard Depardieu). A story about the fatal attraction between a man and a woman becomes the story of the man's destruction by the woman, simply because Truffaut keeps us at a distance from her.

In *Sans toit ni loi* Agnes Varda uses Mona's experience of the diegetic space to underscore the gradual alienation of the homeless woman, Mona. Initially the heroine's refusal to tie herself down appears as an expression of freedom. But gradually her experience of space becomes more and more constricted. The exploration of diegetic space becomes closed to her as she is repeatedly shut out. Doors are always closing on her. Typically, this exclusion occurs from another character's, or from the narrator's point of view rather than from Mona's: the convent door shuts Mona out while the camera remains on the inside; and the shepherd's wife closes her door against Mona while the camera takes a neutral position. On her last trip to buy bread, Mona comes upon a village where everyone is shutting up doors and windows against the celebrants of the wine festival, who are capturing people and smearing them with the dregs. She becomes their sacrificial victim. Her two final refuges, a phone booth and a radish greenhouse, are both open (their walls are transparent) and thus leave her exposed. The wide open spaces of her exploration finally become a trap for her. On her way back from the village, she stumbles and falls into a ditch where she freezes to death.

PERFORMATIVE SPACE: FILM AS SPEECH ACT

In its orientation toward the spectator, my analysis of film space has tacitly assumed that he or she is implicated in what Stephen Heath has called "the *there* of the image." The presence of the image calls forth the active mental construction of the viewer. Heath puts it this way: "Cinema is not a vision but a circuit of vision, the overlay in which the look of the camera and the look of the eye come together."[10]

I have also stated, in the previous chapter, that the spectator will almost always identify with the position of the camera-narrator. Therefore, in order for a strong identification with a character to be felt, the camera must show the character's reflective or projective point of view.

Finally, I brought up some of the complications arising from the reading of conventional narrative films by women spectators. I argued that women typically identify with three different foci in the narrative. In the first place, they are encouraged to identify with the female star as an idealized, and sexually desirable, version of themselves; secondly they identify with the male characters who carry the story line; and thirdly with the landscape through which the male protagonist pursues his goals (reiterating the classic position that women are "means to an end"). The powerlessness implicit in that third identification is one that, narratively, is often represented by the character's silence: the silence of Oharu when scolded by the Matsudaira Clan for becoming a courtesan and prostitute, the silence of Lisa who dares not tell Sebastian Brandt who she is. Oharu and Lisa never break out of being part of the landscape that the male characters traverse as they pursue their life stories.

I want now to describe some situations where that silence becomes the site of a special resistance—a strength rather than a weakness. And, since I have linked it to a particular experience of the diegetic space in film—the passive identification with the landscape—I want to continue to explore that resistance in spatial terms. A few films have explored the idea of opening up the diegetic space itself to represent the site of women's resistance to domination.

Borrowing a term from the philosopher J. L. Austin, we might call the use of film language in these instances "performative." Austin used the term to describe utterances that, when spoken in appropriate circumstances, constitute acts (for instance, "I do" spoken in traditional marriage ceremonies, or "I christen you the Queen Elizabeth," when breaking a champagne bottle against the prow of a new ship). In applying this term from Austin I am suggesting that the films themselves become part of a transforming discourse capapble of restructuring the relation of the female subject to the social space. In this way they fulfill the conditions for what Heath has called "politically consequent" films.[11] They help to forge this new relationship, to make it possible, by representing it. Because they mainly use the characters' new relation to the diegetic space to make their point, I use the term *performative space* to describe their frame-breaking discourse.[12] In performative space the realistically portrayed diegetic space becomes the locus of the women characters' subjectivity—not the subjectivity of dual narration, nor an objective correlative of how the characters feel (as in the examples by Bergman, Allen, and Varda given above), but the locus of a struggle for power. The victory of the women creates them as fully enfranchised individuals. In the two examples below, a film by Marguerite Duras and another by Peter Handke, the women characters retreat to the domestic space with which they have traditionally been identified. Yet they use that reclaimed space to mount an attack on the men who seek to dominate them.

In Marguerite Duras's *Nathalie Granger*, Nathalie is a little girl who has been thrown out of school because of her violence toward the other children. The only shots of the film from outside the space of the house where Nathalie lives with her mother Isabelle, another woman, and her daughter Florence are shots of the interview between the school's headmistress and the two mothers. During the course of the day, Isabelle Granger decides not to send her away to another school, but the decision is not reached through discussion. The narrator shows us the decision being made by the physical bonding of Nathalie and Isabelle as they stand together watching the other mother and daughter cleaning the pond; the mother moves slightly closer to her daughter in the film frame (Figs. 34–35). Even though they do not touch, the arrangement of the shot suggests the mother's feeling her way into her daughter's resistance. This moment of subjectivity is entirely presented in spatial terms—in the proximity of Nathalie and Isabelle, in their shared moment at the edge of the pond.

34–35. Mother-daughter bonding: moving closer in space. (Marguerite Duras, *Nathalie Granger*)

In another scene, the camera shifts between a hesitant washing machine salesman, who appears to forget his lines whenever the camera is turned on him, and the two women sitting opposite him. Here the spatial arrangement is confrontational; the narrator suggests that the women are sitting in judgment on the man (Figs. 36–37). He has gained entrance into their house (their space), but he proves unequal to dominate the situation. Their attention is entirely directed toward *him*, while he continues to recite the broken lines of his unsuccessful sales talk. Their final verdict, "You are not a traveling salesman," represents their judgment that he has not played his male role in a believable fashion; retrospectively, his spatial position may be read as equivalent to an actor on a stage. The women refuse to "believe" in the man's act; they refuse to acknowledge his right to represent anything. This is the cause of his subsequent psychological crisis: he later returns to the house and confesses the history of his professional and personal failures. It is as though the women have unmasked him.

Nathalie Granger manifests a diegetic space in which the women exist in complete integrity, outside the feminine masquerade that defines them in the world of men. As E. Ann Kaplan has said: "Duras's camera emphasizes the separation of the female inner, and male outer, worlds; the house-versus-street polarity becomes a metaphor for the different modes of being that characterize women and men in current society."[13]

The exploration of what I have called performative space is often mediated by sound; for sound, if used as an additional source of information and not just as a repetition of the image track, can do much to liberate the viewer's experience of the film space from the strictures of classical narrative. Mary Ann Doane speaks of such sound as a "place" where alternative modes of representation might be explored.[14] In *Nathalie Granger*, the women's space is also defined by sounds: the sound of the two little girls playing the piano serves as a parallel for the interior, ludic space which the women know so well how to defend by their silence. Appeals from the outside world cannot violate it, since the women are prepared to defend it even against rationality; to get rid of a caller who has dialed a wrong number, one of them explains (over the telephone): "There is no telephone here." *Nathalie Granger* uses the masculine voice of a radio announcer as a contrast to the space defined by the women as they perform their daily tasks about the house. The presentation of this space as being invaded by a male voice does much to underscore the female identity of the arranger. Even the radio story is the story of the capture of two escaped murderers. When the salesman physically invades the house somewhat later, his discourse is contrasted with their mute indifference. It is a strategy of resistance that leaves the spectator with the impression that he or she has intimately lived through several hours of these women's lives by sharing their experience of space.

If *Nathalie Granger* shows a space which has already been won by women, Peter Handke's *The Left-Handed Woman* exemplifies the struggle women must

36–37. Resistance to invasion: the women sit in judgment (Jeanne Moreau, Lucia Bose, and Gérard Depardieu). (Marguerite Duras, *Nathalie Granger*)

go through to find their space, turning the woman's silence into a coherent statement about her position in a society dominated by language and by masculine presence. The mastery of language is equated with the body-language of oppression, as a passage occurring both in Handke's novel and the film suggests: the father, explaining to his son how he achieves domination in business meetings, says: "First I make my victim sit in a corner, where he feels helpless. When I speak, I thrust my face right into his. If my caller is an elderly person, I speak very softly to make him think his hearing has suddenly failed him. It's also important to wear a certain kind of shoes, with crepe soles, like these that I'm wearing: they're power shoes. And they have to be polished until they glow. One has to emanate an aura of mystery. But the main thing is the intimidating face . . . this is my power stare, with the help of which I hope to become a member of the board soon."[15]

Against this intimidating presence, the person whom Handke's narrator, throughout his novel, calls only "the woman" seeks to define her own space and existence. In the film version of *The Left-Handed Woman* he calls to his aid, in the definition of the woman's alternate, autonomous space, a film language that speaks from outside the dominant Hollywood narrative mode, creating a film, as one critic puts it, "unthinkable in America."

Handke's tripartite grouping of his film into sequences titled "March-April-May" is consistent with this evolution, as is his insistence on mundane household tasks which are focused on for their ability to take up time. The spectator gets to know the heroine not through her decisions in moments of crisis (the Aristotelian indicator of character) but through her atypical ways of performing typical household duties. Her throwing away all the food in the refrigerator, dumping the typewriter on the floor, falling asleep at a silent Ozu film—all these become indices of her negativity, her withdrawal and refusal, at the beginning of her revolt, to continue employing the objects of the world in the traditional way. During the first part of the film when her husband returns from a trip, takes her out to dinner, and spends the night with her at a hotel, Handke does not even have her speak. The husband's voice, the voice of presence, seeks to dominate: "I've never felt so united with you . . . I feel a magical power and I'm so happy." Her first word is one of severance and denial: "I've suddenly had a strange idea . . . I suddenly had the illumination that you were going away from me. That you were going to leave me alone. Yes Bruno, that was it. Go away. Leave me alone. Forever."

In this film the woman's silence helps her to define a new relation to objects. Loneliness and withdrawal into self are conveyed by closeups of a dripping faucet, a bucket. In the isolation that follows her stripping away of her former life, these images reflect the complete stasis of her emotions—a sort of zero point that must be reached before the change can occur.

At the end of *The Left-Handed Woman*, a new reality begins to shape itself. In cinematic terms where the loss of language is translatable into a loss of sight, regaining language is the same as learning a new perception. "I'm starting to see again," says one of the women guests at a party in the woman's house. Like

Riva in *Hiroshima mon amour*, the return to normality translates into a return to the sensory world. At the end of Handke's novel, his heroine begins to draw; she has found a new visual language that absolves her from silence. His film heroine, also, reaches a realization of self that is expressed in more cinematic terms: "Haven't you noticed that there is only space for the person who brings his [sic] own space with him?" Marianne, his heroine, is someone who conquers her own space and thus earns the right to exist in her own time.

Performative space allows a spectator experience that does not rely on the simple transposition of male to female roles; instead the full implications of the woman character's experience of space are explored. For the male spectator, this has the effect of providing for him that double identification with the diegetic characters and with the diegetic space which heretofore has been the special province of women. These films speak for a kind of women's experience that is not "for women only," since any attempt to essentialize the historical experience of women as peculiarly "feminine" must be resisted. Simply, in taking these films seriously we can learn something about the experience of space which has often been the locus of women's struggle.

In conclusion it should be noted that the independence achieved by the women characters in these films is not without ambiguity, since it is represented by the active reclaiming of domestic space, the traditional locus of the house-wife.[16] It is exciting to imagine a film in which the woman character would move outside the home, performatively creating her space as she moved through the narrative. This would be an extremely difficult film to make, since it would necessitate the construction of a new relation between the subject and her environment literally at every step. As Tania Modleski argues, "the performative and mimetic aspects of texts mutually reinforce each other, representation pro-ducing reality and reality affirming representation."[17] In performing a new relation between the character and her space, such a film would break the frames of our normal perception and ultimately have a positive influence on reality itself.

PART FOUR

GENDER

One of the experiences that films allow is the pleasure of identification. Psychology tells us that the child begins to identify with others at a very early stage, and that identifications play a large part in determining personality. When the child becomes a reader and film spectator, transient identifications with the characters of fiction continue to influence personal development. In this final section, I examine the way that film fictions help to produce individuals as gendered subjects, that is as persons who develop social attitudes toward their sexual identity.

So far cognitive theory has had little to say about the different readings caused by variations in gender, class, race, and cultural context. In cognitive psychology, the work of Lawrence Kohlberg in *Child Psychology and Childhood Education* stands out as an exceptional contribution to the question of gender identification by children.

In the next two chapters I will be examining the manner in which commercial films tend to reinforce stereotypes about gender roles, which, in our society as in every other, are the result of cultural formations. The reinforcement comes both from the stories themselves and from the way the films play on the unconscious fantasies of the spectator. This should hardly be surprising, given the fact that the fictional worlds of film are outgrowths of our literary and cultural heritage. Still, the buried attitudes that influence every phase of cinematic production are well worth exploring.

Gender identity, as a social construction, is of course not synonymous with sexual identity. Our concept of "femininity" has changed a lot since Freud wrote in his *New Introductory Lectures* that "we regard women as weaker in their social interests and as having less capacity for sublimating their instincts than men." It is striking, nevertheless, that our culture forces us to think in terms of gendered dichotomies. Catherine Clément and Hélène Cixous have set some of these out in their book *La Jeune Née* (recently translated as *The Newly Born Woman*):

activity/passivity
sun/moon
culture/nature
day/night
father/mother
head/heart
thought/feeling
logos/pathos

In *Reflections on Gender and Science*, Evelyn Fox Keller explains that these binary divisions were not always regarded as opposite and irreconcilable poles. Alchemical science, which laid the stress on the fusion of male and female elements into a whole, offered an alternative to the mechanical model that replaced it in the seventeenth century. Interestingly, it was surrealism that tried to revive the alchemical metaphor in our century. André Breton regarded the androgyne, a fusion of "masculine" and "feminine" qualities, as the ideal.

In my first chapter, I argue that the recent film *E.T.* gives a picture of "masculinity" that parallels the treatment of "femininity" in *The Wizard of Oz*. Children watching these films are bound to come away with very conservative ideas of gender identity. Moreover, the narrative strategy of the films and the fascination children are bound to feel while under the spell of the film apparatus makes it very difficult for them to develop a critical attitude toward the films' messages. My analysis of two popular children's films situates them within the literary and cultural framework of children's fairy tales, familiar territory to young viewers. I demonstrate how each film works on children's unconscious fantasies, binding them to traditional gender models.

The film star Catherine Deneuve is the focus of my second chapter. Here I examine the way in which mechanical metaphors of desire and sexuality have dominated the portrayal of the film actress. These metaphors, I argue, have their roots in the industrial revolution and are pervasive in the sociology, psychology, and literature of our times. Changing the way we conventionally "script" ourselves as male or female will therefore require a fundamental re-evaluation of our social and intellectual heritage.

Far from being works which "break the frame" of these conventions, the films discussed in the fourth and final section are complicit in reinforcing social norms. In my conclusion, therefore, I suggest some ideas for future films that could critically explore the problem of gender.

CHAPTER

7

SCRIPTING CHILDREN'S MINDS
E.T. and *The Wizard of Oz*

Although separated by more than forty years, *The Wizard of Oz* and *E.T.* have in common the fact that they are two of the most popular films of all time. More interesting than the circumstance that the films made money—a lot of it—is the fact that they are movies that children (and some adults, too!) insist on seeing many times. In this sense the film viewing experience recreates the repetition that Freud and others have seen as central to the activity of play in children.[1] Moreover, the psychologist Jean Piaget links children's play to unconscious fantasies; it is a form of acting out psychic conflict.[2] Play is "symptomatic" in that it is one way that repressed feelings or ideas surface—yet another return. It is very intriguing, in this perspective, that both films deal with a departure and return: Dorothy is removed from home by a tornado and must find the way home; E.T. (his initials stand for Extra-Terrestrial) is abandoned by his "mother" spaceship and must also find a way to summon it so that he can go back home. Probably the explanation for the success of these films lies with the fact that they dramatize some unconscious fantasies that children feel to be primordial; these films speak to the deepest part of themselves.

As fictions, *E.T.* and *The Wizard of Oz* engage their viewers in a type of play that fiction supremely allows: the play of identification. That is to say, the films mediate the experience of identifying with various characters, allowing *playful* and hypothetical identifications that repeat in some way the important identifications in life which have led to the child's formation of self. Moreover, as myth, the films evoke the question which is of central importance to children: the myth of origin.[3] Although they do not answer this question, the films provide a coherent narrative that stands as a fictional answer, one that children can accept because of their nostalgic sense of past. Both films, then, are narrative creations by which children are expected to perform a cognitive act.

Film has often been described as a voyeuristic medium, enabling the viewer, in the relative privacy of the darkened theater, to enjoy the vicarious enactment of unconscious wishes. The absence of live actors paradoxically creates a stronger feeling of presence in the viewer, who easily identifies with the characters of the fiction and is pulled mentally into the narrative space by various cognitive strategies employed by the filmmakers.[4] The fascination of a film, its "hold" on the spectator, depends to a great extent on how close it comes to portraying material from the viewer's own unconscious. Moreover, if such material is conveyed in a cryptographic form, the way our dreams are, we are likely to gain additional pleasure from reflecting on what we have seen, in an attempt to puzzle it out. As will be seen in the case of *E.T.* and *The Wizard of Oz*, the fictional disguise enables the films to become vehicles for a number of scenarios which employ, to varying degrees, material from the unconscious. The concealment of unconscious fantasies is necessary because no one wants to confront their unconscious wishes outright; even in dreams, these are concealed by mechanisms Freud described as "the dreamwork."

As narratives, *The Wizard of Oz* and *E.T.* appear as a complicated fabric of possible meanings, all of which must be "unpacked" as it were and sought for below the surface. Like the story of a recounted dream, their surface coherence is only a manifest content under which latent unconscious material is concealed. Moreover, there are a number of different condensed meanings, not all of which are consistent with one another. This should not surprise us, since we know from Freud that in the unconscious there is no logical contradiction, nor is there any sense of linear time. Indeed the multiplicity of cognitive schemas that the films activate accounts for their appeal and success, what Peter Brooks has called the "force of fiction."[5]

From the perspective of the influence of any given film on a spectator, a psychoanalytic approach to film should emphasize not the hypothetical mental state of the characters in the film, nor that of the film's creator (who may be more or less unconscious of the set of significations I am about to propose), but rather the constructions that the film activates in the viewer. These constructions should be visualized as various schemas, nested one within the other, that are playfully considered by the viewer. Piaget provides my model for the constructive reading that includes conscious as well as unconscious thoughts: "The nesting of schemas as seen in symbolic thought is no more mysterious than that to be found in any work of intelligence. The unconscious is everywhere, and there is an intellectual as well as an affective unconscious. This means that it does not exist as a 'region,' and that the difference between consciousness and the unconscious is only a matter of gradation or degree of reflection."[6]

Watching film is a form of play that we should take seriously. Psychologist Lawrence Kohlberg has explained the cognitive import of children's play, in which the "play attitude is not ignoring of reality, it is not 'primary process,' nor is it primarily motivated by untamed drives of sex and aggression. Rather, children's play, like their 'work' attitudes toward the world, is directed toward mastering reality."[7]

In our culture films are not just objects of consumption. They are formative, in that they help to "script" children's minds: they are a factor in determining the attitudes and behavior children will develop in life. Part of the popularity of the two films I have chosen to discuss is no doubt due to the fact that they deal with issues of gender identity and role playing that are central to children.

The films' ideology in relation to these issues is not only a matter of content; it is part of their narrative structure and system of visual representation. The concepts I will be using to unravel these many-layered messages will include cognitivist Roger Schank's notion of scripts and their relation to learning, and psychologist Donald Spence's exploration of narrative truth in psychological development.

To begin with, both films lay the groundwork for the ideological messages by creating an atmosphere of what Donald Spence has called "narrative truth"—a mix of plausibility, familiarity, and repetition.[8] The plausibility of both narratives is strengthened by the fact that both are stories of going home that children can identify with: Dorothy wants to return to Kansas and Elliot wants to help E.T. get back to his own planet. They are also stories about the resolution of cognitive conflict and thus replay the real-life contradictions that children are called upon to resolve in passing through successive stages of their cognitive development; they call upon the faculties of what psychologist Lawrence Kohlberg calls "the young child as philosopher." For instance, Elliot must decide to help E.T. over the competing demands of adult authority, and Dorothy must decide to put aside her immediate goal in order to help her three friends, the lion, the tin woodsman, and the scarecrow.

The familiarity of the stories is assured by intertextual references: Peter Pan is a continuous motif in *E.T.*, whereas *The Wizard of Oz* is well-stocked with such fairy-tale staples as wicked witches, the little animal as helper (Toto), the fairy godmother, and magic shoes.

The narrative truth of both films hides a deeper script about gender identification. By script I am referring to Roger Schank's notion of clustered concepts that typically occur together in narratives of a given culture; scripts are also associated with plans or goals.[9] I shall argue that *E.T.* encourages children to identify traditional, phallocratic behavior as part of the cognitive growth and development of boys, while the fairy tale Dorothy dreams illustrates her coming to terms with the double-bind of femininity. That double-bind is expressed by the syllogism that gets her back to Kansas: "If I ever go looking for my heart's desire again, I won't look any further than my own back yard; because if it isn't there, I never really lost it to begin with."[10] Thereafter she will be locked into her role as woman; either she has never left or lost "home," or it is all she can hope to find by leaving it. The film's technological profusion and visual and verbal display are marshalled in the service of this simple restatement of a familiar script.

The *Wizard of Oz* must be read backwards against this closure to demonstrate its avoidance of the question of what Dorothy really wants; for the question of what women "want" is said to have elicited a frustrated outburst from Freud himself. What Dorothy wants cannot be solved by wizardry, the way the desires of the men can in the film. In the face of such mystery, she does what women have always done—she gives up her claim. The effect of the film is to dramatize this lesson that, it suggests, all little girls must learn. Its appeal comes from its familiar ring and its parcel of truth about the fate of women in the social construction of reality.

What *does* Dorothy (woman) want? Simply to be able to arrange the external world according to her own definitions of "rightness," rather than being manipulated into a position of what is good "for her" by others. At the beginning of the film, she is terrified by the prospect of losing her dog Toto to Miss Gulch, who threatens to confiscate him. Toto has been tearing up Miss Gulch's vegetable garden, a threat to the only fertility available to spinsterhood. That fertility, however, is, by implication, already compromised (a gulch is a negative image of the fruitful earth). In the Oz sequence, the bad witches of the east and west are associated with winter—the forest ruled by the witch of the west is a bleak autumnal forest, and the winged monkeys wear death-like masks. From the beginning, Miss Gulch (who later reappears in the guise of the wicked witch of the west) illustrates the terrifying image of what happens to women if they do not become "real" women and marry. The spinster is an embodiment of what psychologist Melanie Klein has called the "phallic mother" who withholds rather than giving, and she represents the chaos that ensues when women are not kept in their place: even the law is afraid of her, and she is able to obtain a court order for Toto's removal. The wizard, in the dream transformation of this state of affairs, is equally afraid of the wicked witch of the west who compromises his power. His condtion for helping Dorothy and her companions is that she bring him the witch's all-too masculine broomstick.

The Oz story can be read as Dorothy's navigation between two female role models who reproduce almost literally what Melanie Klein has described as the splitting of the mother-imago into good and bad.[11] It helps that Dorothy is an orphan, so that these two sides of the mother are not contradicted by any fictional representation of her "real" mother. According to Klein, both girls and boys initially turn away from their mothers when they experience oral frustration at the time of weaning; both turn toward their fathers. The boy does so with a sense of identification; but the girl's relation to the father is one of jealous rivalry with the mother. This, combined with the original frustration, initially leads the girl to create a cruel mother-imago that becomes part of her superego—a punishing mother.[12] When the girl passes into the genital stage, that image is counterbalanced by the image of a kind and bountiful mother.

Miss Gulch is a frightening image of what Dorothy might become if she continues to make her insistent demands. Like the spinster, Dorothy sows chaos into the ordered fertility of the farm, interrupting her aunt and uncle who are trying to save some baby chicks, and keeping the men from their work by falling in the pigpen. Is it any wonder that no one listens to her? Like Miss Gulch, she is unable to see that others are more important than herself. Nevertheless, the film's strategy is to make the viewer feel sorry for Dorothy (initially) and then to show, through the Oz parable, that her claims were wrong-headed.

Dorothy runs away when Toto returns, having escaped from the spinster's bicycle basket. She scoops him up and runs away from the farm into the hands of Professor Marvel. But if Miss Gulch represents one kind of death, the Professor is another. A death's head actually ornaments the door of his trailer—a visual warning of what might happen to overly independent little girls. She is caught in between: there is literally no exit. In the first of a series of manipulations, the "Professor" decides what is good for her and sends her back to Auntie Em.

The tornado arrives just in time to objectify, by external forces, what amounts to the girl's catastrophic discovery of the claims she must give up. It is not only that she must learn to allow the equal claims of others; she must learn to subordinate her own. Knocked out by a flying shutter that has been loosened by the wind, Dorothy now embarks on an elaborate imaginary journey in which she rationalizes her farewell to childhood. When she returns, she will no longer be the center even of her own universe.

As a myth, the story that Dorothy experiences addresses itself to the following question: how can she find a space for herself when both spaces, home and away from home, seem to offer no place for any kind of claim? In the world of her dreams, her frustrations of powerlessness are transmuted into symbols of power: her house crushes the wicked witch of the West and she is welcomed as a liberator. Her weakness becomes a form of protection and allies her with the fertility she was in danger of compromising back in Kansas.

"Home," the endpoint toward which the fantasy moves, starts out by crushing the wicked witch of the east, so that Dorothy opens the door of her farmhouse onto a technicolor celebration of spring in Munchkinland. In the dream transformation of the (black-and-white) world of Kansas, the dwarves function as displacements of the baby chicks, which she has now managed to save by killing the witch. The rest of her trials, which happen along the way of her attempts to get back to Kansas, will be similar expressions of her identification with the "good mother" figure and will depend similarly on the exercise of feminine symbols: the protective red shoes (a severed limb is perceived as a male organ, but shoes "fit" the foot and are hence perceived as female), and water (associated with birth). In her fantasy, Dorothy herself becomes a goddess of fertility along with the focus of her identification, the good witch of the north. The position of witch of the south is, after all, unclaimed; and if winter and fall are the province of the bad witches, spring and summer are still there to be shared by the two good ones. The tornado, which was a threat to summer, is thus overcome at the level of seasonal symbolism as well.

I think it important to stress that Dorothy's power is as destructive as that of the wicked witches; the point of her allegorical journey is that she must learn to bend this destruction to constructive aims, e.g. the encouragement of men. For she helps each of her companions to believe that they have the phallus they long for, in whatever form it takes. What the wizard gives them is an appendage (a diploma, a clock, a medal), but it is only through her—service to a lady—that these signs gain their true significance. In this way the film allegorizes and justifies through what Donald Spence might call its "narrative fit" the power relations of phallocratic society. The three have by then already proven themselves as resourceful, courageous, and loving by helping Dorothy. And, by allowing herself to be served, she also gains her identity as a woman. Men, it seems, have it easy. The scarecrow is *already* smart: he tricks the talking trees into throwing down their apples, and masterminds the attack on the witch's castle. The tin man already has a heart: he cries so much about Dorothy's plight in the wicked witch's castle that his friends have to admonish him to stop ("Don't cry now; we haven't got the oil can and you're squeaking enough already"). And the lion actually leads the way in the steep ascent up the witch's cliff. All the men need is to be reassured that they already possess what they want. Freud suggests as much: men's lives, after the resolution of the Oedipus complex in which they learn to displace their love for mother or sister onto an external object, stretch out in uncomplicated fashion, offering them the possibility of one conquest (intellectual, military, or sentimental) after another.

The film's celebration of phallocratic male scripting is echoed in the wizard's words: he calls universities "seats of learning where *men* go to become great thinkers" and speaks of "*men* who are called heroes" and "*men* who do nothing all day but do good deeds". It is true that Dorothy unmasks the wizard and reveals him as a small, powerless man. But this does not lead to a solution of her problems, for he is unable to take her back to Kansas. Notice that his balloon can take *him* there—a man—even though he shouts in parting that he doesn't even know how it works. Like the heart, the brain, and the courage bestowed on the other men, this power, too, is hardly explainable because it rests on a myth. And women, after all, must not find out too much lest the wizardry of the phallus be totally unmasked (that would mean revolution). There is a strong implication that Dorothy's exposure of the wizard is like the witnessing of a primal scene, exciting because forbidden.[13] Yet, since the wizard's machinery may be taken as a metaphor for the technology of cinema itself, everything depends on the film's disavowal of its own self-exposure, and the mystery is quickly reinstated. Like the masquerading woman Dorothy will become, the film charms and seduces by its appeal to the irrational and disarms the viewer.

Before Dorothy returns to Kansas, the wizard departs, leaving her three companions in charge of Oz: whether they are perceived by the viewer as men or as surrogate children Dorothy has created with the wizard-as-father, the fact remains that she internalizes a male standard in her ideal fantasy world.[14] Dorothy learns nothing except the substitution of her masculinity complex (her demanding attitude) for feminine strategies of attention-getting through mothering, falling sick, and acting helpless. She wakes up in Kansas in bed, a prediction of either future neurasthenia or childbearing. As before, no one listens to her.

In her discussion of the way the child splits the nurturing and withholding mother into two personae, Melanie Klein is at pains to stress the deep-seated roots of that split in culture. In the Greek myth of Orestes, the two facets of the mother are represented as the persecutory fates (the Erinyes) and the protecting goddesses (the Eumenides). If Dorothy, like Orestes, is guilty of killing the bad mother (the first wicked witch), she must expiate the guilt associated with that destructiveness (exemplified in the projection of her harsh superego in the persona of the wicked witch of the west) in order to be accepted by society. In Aeschylus, that expiation is mediated by the goddess Athena, who has no mother. Like Athena, the witch Glinda stands for the "wise and mitigated" superego.[15] She thus provides an identification for Dorothy who adopts her as a fantasy mother.

Dorothy's compromise fantasy allows her to adopt a new identity as a royal child living among commoners. Hereafter she will masquerade, turning her "true self" inward. Freud has described the little boy's "family romance," a fantasy in which he attributes to himself a high-born father, as a way out of the guilt arising from the Oedipus complex: if the man who lives with his mother is not his real father, then it is all right to wish to get rid of him so as to gain possession of his mother. The *Wizard of Oz* suggests the value for girls of fantasizing a high-born mother, a value which does not consist in the simple reversal of the masculine terms of the boy's fantasy. Here the illusion of nobility provides a rationalization for the severe compromise formation necessary to the girl's adjustment to her inferior status in society ("since I am royal, my role is to be kind to my inferiors"). And, whereas Freud speaks of the little girl's masquerade as a means of seducing the father,[16] it would seem to have a more serious consequence: the masquerade becomes a part of women's identity because women are blocked from self-realization. In women, it serves as a necessary and mature defense against what otherwise would be an intolerable position.[17] Ultimately, of course, the masquerade has perverse effects: it turns the exterior into a shell that is easily filled in by men's fantasies, because their love objects are surrogates for earlier object choices.

Frank Baum's original book was far more progressive than the film that was eventually made from it.[18] In 1986 a fundamentalist group of parents in Greenville, Tennessee sued (Mozert vs. Hawkins Public Schools) to protect their children from the harmful influence of the *Wizard of Oz* book on the grounds that it promoted feminist ideas (an excessively independent heroine) and witchcraft.[19] In the film, however, Dorothy is far from being independent. What Dorothy's three companions receive from the wizard is a script; they are automata which can now function "as if" they were genuine (just as everyone else does). And Dorothy too becomes an automaton by her assumption of the feminine masquerade.[20] Everyone, it seems, is condemned to experience at second-hand.

Few children, it may be supposed, can resist the verbal euphoria of the lion's song ("What makes the Hottentot so hot/What puts the ape in apricot"), or such expressions as "gentle as a lizard, clever as a gizzard" (to rhyme with "wizard"), or the wizard's description of the tin woodsman as a "clinking clanking, clattering collection of caliginous junk," all of which anticipate the playful use of language that has been so successful on children's TV programs (*Sesame Street*, for one). If play has been shown by Piaget to be close to the child's unconscious, then this play on language is equally close to the mechanisms of dreamwork: condensation and displacement in the examples above, figurative representation in the "horse of a different color" which actually changes color during the friends' brief ride, or the scarecrow who is told "they really knocked the stuffing out of you." As harmless as these word games seem, they set up a suspension of rational defenses that feeds into the child viewer's identification with Dorothy. This identification becomes a learning experience in which role models are reinforced.

Now just try, for a minute, to rewrite this film for a male protagonist, a young boy about Dorothy's age. Imagine the following scenario: a boy whom I shall call "Daniel" is threatened with the loss of his dog and a mean spinster comes to take the dog away. Dan doesn't run away from home because by the time he is Dorothy's age, he is expected to stand up to aggression, shoulder responsibility, and take part in the work of the farm. If he does leave home in anger (rather than run away), it is these responsibilities that he feels guilty about. The tornado comes and Dan lands in Oz, killing the wicked witch. Glinda appears and Dan sees her as a fantasy replacement for mom. To win her approval, he sets off toward Oz, wearing the witch's magic belt. On the way, he meets three companions who follow him because they recognize him as a leader. Dan exposes the wizard, thus gaining the phallus for himself. However, rather than remain content in Oz, he returns to earth to carry out his responsibilities to his fellow men. The transposition of the Oz story brings some of the latent sexual content to the surface, but it can be reassimilated by other familiar fairy tales. As we shall see, gender transposition won't work in the case of Steven Spielberg's E.T., which does an equally good job of scripting a conventional "narrative truth" for boys.

Even before E.T. enters the scene, we find out that Elliot's father has left the mother and three children and is in Mexico with another woman. The mother is having a hard time controlling the three children, Elliot, Michael, and Gertie, who are competing for the mother and against each other. As middle child, Elliot is the most fiercely competitive, condescending toward his younger sister and resentful of his brother. Elliot is a loner and seems cut off from masculinity by his older, more prepossessing brother and by the absence of the role model a father might provide.

In E.T. the boy has a "secret" that makes him special, gives him power over others. Here E.T.'s phallic shape comes into play; as one analyst has pointed out, children never mistake E.T.'s gender for anything but male (Fig. 38).[21] Elliot's special relation to E.T. endows him with superiority, not only over the little sister, whose frightening screams cause an alarming tumescence in the extra-terrestrial, but also over his classmates, whose attitude changes to one of respect and co-conspiracy against the adults. Needless to say, the absence of Elliot's father makes it easier for Elliot to gain the ascendancy at home.

The multiple incarnations of E.T. in Elliot's (and the viewer's) fantasies amount to a complex web of condensations, displacements, and figurative representations characteristic of the unconscious. Woven into the more superfi-

38. E.T. and Elliot (Henry Thomas). (Steven Spielberg, *E.T.*)

cially visible narrative, this unconscious material becomes subtly manipulative of the child spectator's wishes and fantasies.

E.T. is a displacement of the paternal phallus, as can be seen by Elliot's desire to acquire E.T. for himself and to use him exclusively against his brother and sister in order to gain leadership of the family. In a comic scene in which the mother fails to see E.T. in the kitchen and living room, Elliot shows that he secretly has control over his mother. The possession of E.T. also gives him very real powers, and he suddenly gains a peer group (like the one his brother has at the beginning of the film) which asserts itself against adult authority. Through E.T. the boys are able to outrun the police by flying on their bicycles and to outwit a team of scientists who descend upon the home to study the extra-terrestrial.

By combining Freud with Piaget's theory of stages in the child's development, one doesn't need to see this sexual content as more "primal," but as corresponding to topics that young children are especially preoccupied with. Kohlberg has produced evidence to show that, in his words, the six-year-old boy is a "full-fledged male chauvinist" whose concept of gender identity actually becomes more flexible as he grows older.[22]

E.T.'s situation in the narrative is also a condensed metaphor for birth. The opening scene is shown from the point of view of E.T.'s confused consciousness as he realizes he is "left behind" on earth. Elliot subsequently becomes the "parent" of E.T. Finally, in a scene near the close of the film the whole house

39. E.T.'s magical touch. (Steven Spielberg, *E.T.*)

is enclosed in a womblike plastic structure attached to large hoses (the birth canal). Within this "womb," E.T., who is assumed to have died, experiences a rebirth. Elliot's role becomes that of facilitator, ushering him down the "canal" and conveying him in a bicycle basket (recapitulating the story of Moses) to the place of rendezvous with his "mother" spaceship.

To the extent that Elliot identifies with E.T. as foundling, he is excused from appropriating the phallus at his father's expense. E.T.'s telepathic communication with Elliot suggests that he is, in one schema, Elliot's double and that his birth is also Elliot's (witness the real grief when the scientists "separate" their twin existence; Elliot says to E.T.: "You must be dead because I can't feel anything anymore"). Elliot's internalization of his companion's feelings stands for the viewer's identification with Elliot, a point underscored by the scene in which Elliot's kissing his girl classmate is motivated by E.T.'s identification with characters shown on a TV screen.

As a projection of Elliot's (and the child viewer's) phallic fantasies, E.T. is also a fantasy replacement for dad. In this sense the telepathic TV communication described above is one in which "dad" takes Elliot to the movies once again, as in the old days that the children nostalgically wish for at the beginning of the film.

In order to further disarm the viewer, Spielberg laces the film with intertextual references to other children's tales and films. The Peter Pan story is touched on in several instances; the mother reads the story to Gertie; E.T. is able to cure wounds (Fig. 39) by the touch of his finger ("Tinker Bell will get well," etc.); and E.T., like Peter Pan, enables his friends to fly through the air. The appearance of another surrogate father figure, Yoda, from *The Empire Strikes Back* (of the Star Wars film series) in the form of a child's Halloween disguise is another instance.[23]

The familiarity the spectator feels on experiencing the story of E.T. is created, therefore, by both the unexpected return of repressed unconscious material and citations of familiar stories and films. Another source is cultural memory. E.T. is a romantic hero, untouched by the anxieties and skepticism of modernism and at one with nature.

The appeal to romanticism is necessarily appreciated more by adults than by children. The adult's reaction to the story is one of nostalgia. Through identification with Elliot, he or she is able to become a child again, thus reversing the separation from nature caused by the assumption of rationality. Lest the adult viewer resist the invitation to identify with the boy, an adult surrogate is supplied to authorize that move—he is the scientist who assures Elliot that he is glad the boy met E.T. first.

Against the adult world, E.T. uses the typical weapons of the hero of romanticism; hypnotism, magnetism, telepathy. He fights not men but the split between self and world that prevents him from going "home."[24] There is a strong suggestion that it is E.T.'s communication with Elliot's unconscious that allows him to repair this rift; they save each other. If E.T. is the foundling that appears over and over again in the texts of the romantic era, he makes a foundling of Elliot who is now specially marked to live the life of the imagination.[25] Throughout, *E.T.* is marked by narcissistic euphoria, as Elliot comes to know his own powers through his companion, a metamorphosis of the imagination presaged, in the first family scene, by the symbolic steam rising from the dishwasher and enveloping him in the mists of fantasy, like the locomotive's steam in another cinematic poem to childhood, Jean Vigo's 1933 film *Zéro de conduite*. At the end of the film, Elliot has become the hero-survivor of his own birth and of his family's destructive tyranny. Like H. G. Wells's time-traveler in *The Time Machine*, E.T. takes away with him the flower that will prove his trip to earth was not just the dream that it has been for us, the viewers.

If we try to transpose the gender of the child hero in *E.T.*, some of the latent sexual content I have been discussing easily surfaces. Suppose that little "Ellery" finds the extra-terrestrial and hides him in her closet. She would then have something that her brother doesn't—a phallic pet whom she mothers. E.T. bestows great power on her and becomes her best friend. We have here the beginnings of a revolutionary scenario, for one can't easily imagine E.T. in the silly posture of Dorothy's male companions; the extra-terrestrial is too powerful a helper for the accommodative wishes that Dorothy is limited to in *The Wizard of Oz*. In the right hands, the story could become a feminist parable, although not one that could be produced for the mass market. The idea, on the other hand, that E.T. could be female is made fun of in the film when Gertie attempts to dress him in her doll's clothes—E.T. in drag is a ridiculous

40. E.T. dressed by Gertie. (Steven Spielberg, *E.T.*)

figure (Fig. 40). Entertainment films are expected to reinforce stereotypes, not challenge them. The transformation I have suggested is a way of foregrounding the conventions within which traditional narrative operates; the very real constraints on story-telling become much clearer once we think about changing them by crossing gender lines.

The social conditioning that young audiences undergo as a result of seeing these films should be taken seriously. Freud has stressed how identification plays a role in character formation; this identification can occur with another person (it occurs inevitably with the parent, or parental figure),[26] but also with the characters of fiction.[27] Christian Metz has laid the groundwork for the way the specular relation between filmgoer and film—the absent presence of the actors, which allows the imaginary substitution of self for the "absent presence" of the character fictively embodied on the screen—actually binds the viewer more tightly than the written word into its structures of address.[28] All this suggests that films take part in the formation of the viewer as a subject in society. As subjects in history, we are partly defined by the ideological and discursive formations that surround us. We are already in *The Wizard of Oz* as our children are in *E.T.*

CHAPTER
8

THE MYTH OF THE PERFECT WOMAN
Cinema as Machine Célibataire

In 1985 a statue of the French film actress Catherine Deneuve was chosen to represent "Marianne," the female symbol of France. The French populace themselves were invited to choose from among twenty-four competing statues, to be put up in every *mairie* (local seat of government). The face of Deneuve replaced that of Brigitte Bardot; Deneuve was said to be more representative of the "woman of the 80s."[1] Roland Barthes, who discusses the "myth" of Greta Garbo in his *Mythologies*, would have had much to say about this new addition to the pantheon. For it illustrates dramatically one of the basic tenets of his work: that modern-day myths are symptomatic of commonly held beliefs in our society.

This chapter will examine some of the beliefs surrounding the "star" quality of Deneuve. What follows is not a global analysis of the film star, but one that focuses on a single example. Nevertheless I feel that the effects I will describe are symptomatic of the representation of women and sexuality in the period stretching from the industrial revolution to the present day. Woman's desire, I will argue, is represented as a kind of motor that must be alimented by reserves of male energy; it is seen as a negative force that consumes without fecundity. The female film star is constructed to be the embodiment of that desire. She circulates arbitrarily among men who are helpless to win her permanent attachment. As a result, she is both admired and feared.

This view of the place of women in a mechanized sexual economy has analogies in a variety of other domains. The French philosopher Michel Serres has described the way in which the steam engine, at the time of the industrial revolution, became the master metaphor of the age. According to Serres, the Freudian unconscious and the Marxian theory of the accumulation of capital are seen to be "translations" of one and the same informing mental set, which also gives rise to the appropriate artistic expression in fiction, philosophy, and painting: Zola, Bergson, and Turner.[2] The steam engine metaphor is a metaphor of thermodynamics, and the inclusion of Freud and Marx is explained by the fact that both posit the buildup of pressure (either the repressed unconscious or the suppressed proletariat) which then sets certain compensatory events in motion.

Serres might well have included cinema as a new artistic medium called into being by the imagination of the nineteenth century. Cinema is of particular relevance here as an instance of the cultural product of a given social formation, since, as André Bazin has pointed out, the scientific conditions for the creation of cinema and photography existed long before anyone actually bothered (or needed) to invent them.[3]

What brought cinema into being, finally, was its ability to fulfill a social need for representation. It is important to stress that the cinema is an apparatus whose very existence is predicated on the desire of the spectator. The elementary pleasure that a film gives is that of seeing, the satisfaction of curiosity. As films began to be shown in theaters before audiences, the spectators' desire to "see more" was matched by the development of the narrative film, and by the institutionalization of voyeurism in the erotic content of the cinematic spectacle.

Because of the close ties of the spectacle to box office profitability, the apparatus of cinema has from the beginning been in a position to echo the unconscious fears of society. There is thus a double edge to the motorized version of the erotic in which the female star is represented as a machine or automaton against which the masculine could define itself. On the one hand, this representation expressed the fear that people experienced when dealing with an increasingly mechanized world over which the individual had less and less control. The portrayal of the threatening eroticism of women that appear as robots (as in Fritz Lang's *Metropolis*, 1928) is an instance. On the other hand, the metaphor of mechanization lent concrete form to an unconscious fear in patriarchy: that of the return of the repressed woman in a form that would be difficult to control because it would not be human.

In this guise the mechanical woman represents the threat that the traditional split between science and nature, that came into being in the seventeenth century, might fall apart. As Evelyn Fox Keller states, the mechanical philosophy that gained the ascendancy at that time was expressed in terms of the masculine domination of science over nature, represented as feminine. This polarization of gender, she argues, was required by the economics of the rising industrial capitalism. Specifically, mechanical science replaced the alchemical metaphor for science which was based on the union of male and female elements: "The goal of the new science is not metaphysical intercourse but domination . . . the triumph of those who have been generally grouped together as 'mechanical philsophers' represented a decisive defeat of the view of nature and woman as Godly, as of a science which would accordingly have guaranteed to both at least a modicum of respect."[4]

In the fiction that attends the industrial revolution, the fear of machines found expression in the creation of imaginary "celibate machines" (*machines célibataires*). First coined by the painter Marcel Duchamp to designate his project "The Bride Stripped Bare by Her Bachelors, Even" ("La Mariée mise à nu par ses célibataires, même"), the term has been extended by the French critic Michel Carrouges to include a variety of literary works which depict the machine creations of their protagonists. The imaginary machines are called "bachelor machines" because, unlike industrial machines, they are unproductive. According to Carrouges, "the myth of bachelor machines is a clear signpost for the simultaneous rule of the mechanical and reign of terror."[5] As examples Carrouges cites two novels that I will discuss here, Villiers de l'Isle Adam's *L'Eve future* and Jules Verne's *Le Château des Carpathes*. In addition he mentions some of the machines described in Raymond Roussel's *Locus solus*, in Franz Kafka's "The Penal Colony," in Edgar Allan Poe's "The Pit and the Pendulum," and in Alfred Jarry's *Le Surmâle* (among others).

In order to understand how these machines "operate," we must return to Michel Serres's steam engine metaphor. Serres states that the steam engine has three requirements. In the first place, there must be a difference between two poles of temperature. In the second place, there must be a reservoir of energy. And thirdly, there must be circulation between the reservoir and the machine in order to ensure its operation. In the case of philosophical systems built on the machine model, these elements become quite metaphorical (in Marxian theory, the categories of difference, energy reservoir and circulation are filled by class differences, capital, and revolution; in Freudian theory by repression, the unconscious, and neurotic or psychotic symptoms).[6] In the "bachelor machine," the two poles are sexualized. The "difference" operates between the "male" and "female" parts, whose interaction constitutes its force. As is the case with other machine models (such as the Marxian and the Freudian), the end result may be cathartic or even catastrophic.

There are many reasons for arguing that the "machine célibataire" functions with the force of an epistemic paradigm for an entire system of intersubjective relations that stretch from postromantic ideology into our present cybernetic age (and perhaps even beyond it). I think a strong case can be made for the idea that the structure of desire embodied and encouraged by film spectatorship is furthered by a system of values discernible elsewhere in some literary works as well as in Freudian and Lacanian psychology. Even the current inquiry into artificial intelligence has tended to reinforce existing cognitive typologies rather than to explore the problem of originality (and hence the possibility for change).

Duchamp's "La Mariée mise à nu par ses célibataires, même" ("The Bride Stipped Bare by Her Bachelors, Even") will form the paradigm for my analysis. It is the quintessential "bachelor machine." Moreover, its sexual politics are echoed in the cinematic apparatus of the film star which is the focus of my interest. Standing some ten feet tall, Duchamp's work (also called "The Large Glass") appears as a kind of portal, one of the thresholds of twentieth-century consciousness.

Duchamp's "Large Glass" (Fig. 41) has clearly divided masculine and feminine hemispheres. In the upper portion, "la mariée" is a wasp-like figure that seems to hang by, but also at the same time to generate, a series of frames with amorphous borders—shapes that Duchamp described as the "cinematic

41. Marcel Duchamp, *La Mariée mise à nu par ses célibataires, même*. 1915–23. Oil and lead wire on glass, 109 ¼″ × 69 ⅛″; Philadephia Museum of Art. Bequest of Katherine S. Dreier

blossoming" in the extensive notes he made about the work. Between the "bride" and the lower portion there is a sharp division. Here various male forms, whose geometric shapes are meant to evoke the costumes of various professions, are perched on a kind of Glider which is connected to a Chocolate Grinder. Thanks to the operation of male desire on this machine, the notes say, the bride is "stripped," and releases the "cinematic blossoming" described earlier.[7]

Because the "bride" is both generated by and generates the "cinematic blossoming," she can function as a metaphor for the cinema of spectacle, which uses the female star as the point and focus of representation. The bachelors, in this perspective, become the spectators whose desire fuels the economic possibility of the cinematic machine; they both desire the undressing and pay for it. But much more than cinema is at stake. Duchamp's laying bare of the illusionist workings of art goes a long way toward explaining the complex set of drives and inhibitions that make modern men (and their relations to modern women) conform to the model of the unproductive "machine célibataire," a "closed circuit system," in the words of Michel Carrouges, with little possibility of escape. As Albert Cook points out, Duchamp has represented "a machine that will not work mechanically, and one whose parts are greater, not less, than the sum of the whole."[8] Its avowed purpose—the erotic stripping of the bride— is subverted by the incompatible mechanics of the Glider and the Chocolate Grinder. Among other disjunctive components, Cook notes that the gliders on the Glider "are actually facing the wrong way. . . . If they glided, they would glide right out of the picture in one direction and collide head-on with the Chocolate Grinder on the other."[9]

Duchamp's work thus contains an implicit critique of modern sexuality. Not only will the machine not work, but there is a rigorous separation between the male and female spheres. For literary predecessors to this view of the erotic, we can look to Villiers de l'Isle Adam's *L'Eve future* (1880–86) and Jules Verne's *Le Château des Carpathes* (1892). Both have been discussed as literary metaphors for the birth of the cinema.[10] They also figure prominently in Carrouges's discussion of "machines célibataires."

The opening of *L'Eve future* (*Eve of the Future Eden*, in the excellent translation by Marilyn Gaddis Rose which will be quoted here)[11] finds Thomas Edison musing about his new invention, the phonograph, in a vein that may best be described as the prototype of reader-response criticism. Even if he could capture, retrospectively, some of the great voices of history, he reasons, they would not be considered "real" by modern men, for "it is not the sounds which have disappeared but rather the impressive character attached to them in and by the hearing of ancient peoples" (12). In Edison's terms, sounds, thoughts, and images are determined by *reflection* off the historical subject, who must provide the receptive surface. It follows that Edison's current invention, an ideal woman who, by satisfying every wish of her partner, both physical and mental, will protect him from the snares of human women, cannot truly come into existence until he finds the man for her. The female prototype he has created and which he keeps in a subterranean cavern must be refined by the addition of qualities that will satisfy an individual user's fantasies.

By these meditations Villiers sets the scene for the arrival of Lord Ewald, an English benefactor who declares himself on the brink of suicide because Alicia, the woman he loves, lacks the noble sentiments he admires. Edison finds it a simple matter to entice the aspiring actress into his studio where the form of her body is copied ("photosculpted") onto his prototype model Hadaly, while she is coached to recite lines of poetic dialogue under the mistaken assumption that she has gained a part in a play. These dialogues, engraved on golden records, are set into Hadaly, where they can be activated by the speech of her beloved.

How, then, will Lord Ewald be made to feel that Hadaly is "real"? Edison subjects his friend to what amounts to a "Turing machine" test (A. M. Turing, considered to be one of the "fathers" of artificial intelligence, argued that machine intelligence could be said to be equal to human intelligence if, under certain experimental conditions, you could not tell which was which).[12] At the very moment when Lord Ewald, lured into the garden by Alicia, decides to forgive her for her shallowness and to abandon the robot Hadaly, she reveals herself as Hadaly rather than Alicia; Edison's gamble to replace "intellect by Intelligence" succeeds in fooling the lover, for whom the robot functions as the perfect reflection of his illusions.

Still, Hadaly has to fight for her "life" against the horrified reaction of Lord Ewald. An Eve true to her name, she vanquishes him with seductive logic: "at your despairing cry I agreed to put on the radiant lines of your desire in order to become visible."[13] Like Duchamp's bride, Hadaly is fueled by her bachelor, who is instructed to administer doses of chemicals to keep her joints from rusting—to keep her functioning as a desire-machine. But her sophisticated machinery also causes romantic confusion in her lover who proves himself no longer the master of his illusions. Those illusions, once made flesh, enslave him, as he sets out for Athelwold Castle with his doll in her tightly sealed carrying case—a mahogany coffin similar, perhaps, to the one in which Count Dracula traveled to London. Hadaly is, Villiers suggests, the vampire tamed whom one can turn on and off with a key.[14]

Her ancestry in literature is long. In his thought-provoking study of the myth of the actress from Nerval to Proust, Ross Chambers has shown the importance of the actress as the embodiment of the feminine ideal since the postromantic era. This ideal was predicated on the twin concepts of distance (unattainability) and emptiness (artifice rather than substance). Her emptiness allows her to be "filled in" by the poet: *"elle est une écriture qu'on regarde"* (she is a writing that one contemplates).[15] Written by the man who loves her, she is created by his look, without which she would not exist. In this sense Hadaly is Alicia "filled in" by Lord Ewald's writing, anticipating the spectator's filling in of the essentially blank screen actress. In fact, Villiers has Edison claim that all women worth loving affect a blank expression; their eyes are mere mirrors: "In our day, carefully reared women have acquired a unique glance . . . wherein everyone can find the expression he desires but which allows them to think their own thoughts while appearing to pay profound attention. This glance can be photographed. After all, isn't it just a photograph itself?"[16]

Freud's writings suggest that his model of woman closely corresponds to the myth of the actress as explained by Chambers and illustrated in *L'Eve future*. In one instance, he even states that "woman is different from man, for ever incomprehensible and mysterious, strange and therefore apparently hostile."[17] According to the Freudian model, the little girl adopts the masquerade to attract the father, learning the role she will later play with other men. Of necessity such a role is narcissistic on both sides, since the men will be satisfied to discover in her the mirror image of their desire (like Lord Ewald), and the women are put in the role of performing in order to be loved.[18] What both the literary and the psychoanalytic models expose is a form of mental pathology, as Ross Chambers warns: "To make the actress our 'Muse' is . . . to declare our distance from a culture in which we no longer see anything but a universe of signs, one we *observe* instead of *live*."[19]

Nor are we better served by the Lacanian model. Lacan explains the ability of individuals to identify with others (whether these be parents, role models, characters in fiction or film) with the crucial childhood experience of the "mirror stage"—the first moment in which the child can recognize itself in the mirror. The recognition of self as separate from one's surroundings, he argues, means that one can later project oneself into others. I find it somewhat disturbing that "little men" are mentioned in the mirror stage, but not "little women": "the jubilant assumption of his specular image by the child ('le petit homme') at the *infans* stage, still sunk in his motor incapacity and nursling dependence, would seem to exhibit in an exemplary situation the symbolic matrix in which the *I* is precipitated in a primordial form."[20] After all, what creatures but vampires fail to see themselves in the mirror? My view is that Lacan, like Freud, suspected women of not having an "I" in the sense that men have, since the masquerade dictates that a woman's body is always partial and fragmented, even to herself.

Moreover Lacan's own model of the psyche is a motorized model in which men and women are forever separated. The child learns language by recognizing difference. Language, after all, is structured by differences between the phonetic, grammatical, and spatial arrangement of words. The perception of difference is what allows the child to enter into the axis of what Lacan calls the symbolic. This entry is, however, not a liberation but a confinement. Because the most elementary difference is sexual difference, the acquisition of language is indissolubly linked to the trauma of that discovery (the girl's discovery of her missing penis, the boy's fear of castration). Secondly, the site of language is the site of the "Other" (different from the self). This means that an individual is controlled by language rather than mastering it. Finally, and this is where Freudian and Lacanian theory coincide, the desire for the "Other" can never be fulfilled, since one's love objects are never more than a replacement for an imaginary, lost object (for instance, for the feeling of connection with the mother's breast that one had before the realization of oneself as a separate entity in the mirror stage). The Lacanian model is therefore one of irrecoverable loss, that of the "fall" into language.[21]

In the film actress—the star—the masquerade is most developed, since she is physically absent from the spectatorial space. Here the masquerade affects both mise-en-scène (the placing of the star in exotic settings that become the springboard for the fantasies of the spectator, the star's makeup and "glamorous" image) and montage, through which her body is divided up and delivered to the spectator's gaze by closeups. The ideal beauty of a star like Garbo depends on the anonymity of the mask. Roland Barthes has described the way the Garbo face becomes a form of mimicry: "In spite of its extreme beauty, this face, not drawn but sculpted in something smooth and breakable, that is, at once perfect and ephemeral, comes to resemble the flour-white complexion of Charlie Chaplin, the dark vegetation of his eyes, his totem-like countenance."[22]

A mask, as Chambers has said, is "a sign of the face."[23] The blank face of the screen star is a surface onto which desire is written—she is a construction, an automaton.[24] This is the role Catherine Deneuve plays as Séverine in *Belle de jour* (1967). Though apparently happily married, she constantly puts off the sexual advances of her husband. A year or so after her wedding, she is drawn to prostitution (Fig. 42). A "Madame Anais" becomes her employer, and intiates her into the speciality of the house (Fig. 43), which aims at the mise-en-scène of the sexual fantasies of the clients (somewhat like Jean Genêt's *Le Balcon*). This acting out can be seen as the representation of total cinema, the actress come down off the screen. It is the embodiment of the other, phonetic translation of Marcel Duchamp's "La Mariée mise à nu par ses célibataires, même": The bride stripped bare by her bachelors loves me (m'aime).

The spectator's attempt to follow the plot of *Belle de jour* is complicated by the narrator's unreliability: it is often impossible to tell from whose point of view the film images are presented. As in many other Buñuel films, the events presented may or may not be the dream or fantasy of the one of the characters. One episode that seems particularly problematic in that regard begins in an outdoor café. Séverine is joined by an aristocratic gentleman who alights in front of the of the café in a horse-drawn landau (similar to the one that appears in fantasy scenes where, on the orders of her husband, she is stripped and whipped by coachmen). The aristocrat asks her if she likes money, and then invites her to his chateau to perform a ceremony for which, he says, she will be financially rewarded. The scene now shifts to the landau which is bringing Séverine to the chateau. The ceremony in question turns out to require her to "play dead" while lying in a coffin in the chapel of a chateau, nude except for the most transparent black veil. The aristocrat lies underneath and performs some motions that cause the coffin to shake. It is easy to see in this scene a reenactment of Duchamp's "La Mariée." The "bride," in the coffin above, has effectively been stripped bare; separated from her by the wooden box, the "bachelor" gives himself over to the rhythmical motions of desire. One commentator on Duchamp's work unequivocally qualifies the operations of the treadmill and the chocolate grinder as masturbatory;[25] the indications are just

42. Madame Anais (Geneviève Page) looks over Séverine (Catherine Deneuve). (Luis Buñuel, *Belle de jour*)

43. Séverine learns her trade by looking through a peephole. (Luis Buñuel, *Belle de jour*)

as indicative in this scene. But Buñuel goes farther than Duchamp, suggesting that the "machine célibataire" is driven by death, something beyond the pleasure principle. *Belle de jour* shows up the fallacy of the myth of total cinema, since to desire a reproduction of reality that cannot be distinguished from the original is to embrace a lifeless model—to be in love with death.

Séverine's adventures lead to an unhappy end, or at the very least to the suggestion that the "closed circuit" is one which allows no escape. At Madame Anais's, one of the male clients becomes jealous of her other life. He follows her home and shoots down her husband. To the wheelchair-bound husband a male friend finally reveals the details of Séverine's double life. At the end of the film, the heroine appears to fantasize that the tragic events have not, actually, taken place. In a scene that appears metadiegetic from her point of view, the husband arises from the wheelchair as from a deep sleep. She moves over to the window and hears again the bells of the landau with which the story began.

Buñuel's demonization of the feminine in *Belle de jour* can be attributed to displacement, in which women are blamed for men's frustrated desires. Many literary works, as though in acknowledgement of that fact, show that the men who fall for the "perfect woman" are narcissistic and suicidal. According to Chambers, the "myth of the actress" stemmed largely, in France at least, from the influence of E. T. A. Hoffman's story "The Sandman," which was widely diffused as an opera and play. In this story, Nathanael, the protagonist, witnesses as a boy some alchemical operations performed by his father and a friend, Coppelius. During one of those experiments, Coppelius grabs the boy and threatens to take his eyes. Nathanael later falls in love with an automaton doll fabricated by an eyeglass merchant, Coppola, and his university professor; the professor passes the doll off as his own daughter, and Nathanael falls in love with her when looking at her through a pair of binoculars Coppola sells him.[26] She is born of Nathanael's look, as he observes her through the window of his student quarters.[27] But it turns out this doll has Nathanael's eyes—his love for her amounts to a love of self.[28] When Nathanael discovers the truth about Coppelia, he goes mad. Returning home to his first love, Clara, he seems rehabilitated until catching sight of Coppelius while on top of a tower. His jump (as he shouts Coppelius's sales pitch "eyes, lovely eyes") is reminiscent of the leap of Narcissus into the well.

The theme of Narcissus becomes overt in films that actively foreground the woman as automaton by putting forth a literal robot in her place. In the course of Fritz Lang's *Metropolis* (1928), for instance, the scientist Rotwang has fashioned a robot to replace his lost love, Hel, who married the technological overlord of the city, Joh Frederson. In doing so he has created a machine to respond to his desire in place of the woman who would not. Rotwang gives the robot the bodily form of Maria, the woman to whom the workers look for guidance and consolation (and with whom Joh Frederson's son is in love). The robot Maria persuades the workers to destroy their machines and then parties as a vamp seductress among the men who rule the city. Yet the real Maria, being simply more "ideal" than the robot who replaced her, is no less mechanical. Like the robot, she is a projection of male fantasy—a narcissistic echo of male desire. As Enno Patalas writes, "Invariably, the woman, virgin, mother, whore, witch, vamp is constituted—and de-constituted—under the direction of one of the male characters, which in turn predicates the look of another, or many others, including the spectator."[29]

The narcissistic representation of women as robots is one male defense, as I have said, against both the threat of women's sexuality and the feeling of powerlessness in the machine age. Another possiblity is the replacement of women with fetishistic representations of their bodies or voices as in Jules Verne's *Le Château des Carpathes* (*The Carpathian Castle*). These models do not aspire to be completely lifelike; they are recognized as illusions. Yet they work so well that the viewer is constantly slipping between the awareness that they are constructions and the belief that they are real. As such they replay the structure of disavowal that gives rise to the fetish.

Le Château des Carpathes takes place in Transylvania, where a certain Baron Gortz has retired to his impenetrable castle with a treasured recording of the last performance of his favorite opera singer, La Stilla. The singer had intended to retire from the stage and marry, but she dies of fear upon catching sight of the Baron in the audience. By means of a complex system of mirrors and lights applied to a full-size portrait of the singer, and with the aid of a phonograph, the Baron has been able to recreate her farewell song in the privacy of his chambers. The likeness is so convincing that he fools even the young Count Frank de Télek, her fiancé, who penetrates the castle in the hope of finding La Stilla. This story is fetishistic on two counts: the Baron loves not the woman but her voice, and the young Count is tricked into denying the death of his beloved by the substitution of a mechanical double.

The concept of fetishization in psychoanalysis refers to a mental substitution by the male child for the mother's missing penis; it is a defensive reaction to the perceived threat of castration.[30] For this reason, Christian Metz has argued that while a photograph is more likely to become a fetish, film is more capable of playing on fetishism: "Thanks to the principle of a moving cutting off, thanks to the changes of framing between shots . . . cinema literally plays with the terror and the pleasure of fetishism, with its combination of desire and fear."[31] Fetishism substitutes a safe alternative for the real thing; as such it fits squarely into the system of the machine célibataire and its cinematic clones. It mimes not life, but death, preserving, as Bazin has said, objects in a state of mummification: "For the first time, the image of things is likewise that of their duration, change mummified as it were."[32]

Fetishism is the motivating force behind the Deneuve character in François Truffaut's *Le Dernier métro* (*The Last Metro*, 1980). Marion's role in the play *La Disparue* dramatizes the gaps and holes of the body and of the narrative that is constructed so as to fill in these fissures. Taking place during the Occupation, the film recounts how the Jewish director Lucas Steiner hides in the basement of the theater, continuing to direct the play in secret and to listen

44. Marion (Catherine Deneuve) and Lucas Steiner (Heinz Bennent) in the basement of the theater. (François Truffaut, *The Last Metro*)

in on rehearsals and performances through a loudspeaker mechanism operating through the heating vents (Fig. 44). Like Duchamp's bachelors, he assures the motion of the mechanism that undresses the "bride" on the stage above, even going so far as to orchestrate Marion's affair with her costar Bernard Granger. There is, again, the hint of vampirism as Steiner compares his situation to that of the wife in George Cukor's *Gaslight* (1944), who sees the lights go down mysteriously at night while activities she is unaware of are taking place above her head. Here fetishism affects the "body politic" as well, since the conditions of Steiner's existence are dictated by the German Occupation; the theater of desire functions as a disavowal of political castration, just as the multiple fetishizations of Marion by Steiner and others (who comment on her legs, voice, and photographic image) prevent anyone from seeing her as a fully enfranchised individual.

Finally, we have to consider instances of the bachelor machine metaphor in which women are punished.[33] In psychoanalytic terms, the sadistic response relates to the perception of women as castrated men and to men's fear that they are vulnerable to the same punishment. The defense is to punish women for any infringement on male territory or authority. In cinematic narratives, women are often punished for their active sexual curiosity. As Stephen Heath writes, "If the woman looks, the spectacle provokes, castration is in the air."[34]

In her perceptive analysis of silent films starring Rudolf Valentino, Miriam Hansen has demonstrated that this convention was in place from the inception of Hollywood cinema: "Whenever Valentino lays eyes on a woman first, we can be sure that she will turn out to be the woman of his dreams, the legitimate partner in the romantic relationship; whenever a woman initiates the look, she is invariably marked as a vamp, to be condemned and defeated in the course of the narrative."[35]

Looking is equated with sexual curiosity, and like *The Wizard of Oz*, classical films intimate that women should not know too much. In the horror film, women who have not remained "pure" are allowed projective point-of-view shots of the monster who kills them. As Linda Williams points out, such shots feed on male anxiety by suggesting a tacit alliance between the sexual, desiring woman and the monster that threatens to destroy the rest of the characters (men and "good" women).[36]

A similar split occurs in many films of the 40s that were specifically addressed to a female audience. Typically these films show the projective view of the woman's traditional space—the home—as confining. In many cases, the women seem to be on the brink of insanity (*Gaslight; Now, Voyager*). Mary Anne Doane refers to the women characters' paranoid seeing: "The paradigmatic woman's space—the home—is yoked to dread, the crisis of vision."[37] These films present women who must be cured of looking and reintegrated into the passive role of seeing through men (often the mediating man is a psychiatrist) or being seen (and chosen) by them.

In Tony Scott's *The Hunger* (1982) Deneuve plays the role of a female predator—a bisexual vampire who turns her lovers into vampires as well (Fig. 45). It turns out, though, that only one vampire can be immortal at a time; each of the lovers she converts to vampirism ages prematurely and has to be filed away in one of the coffins she keeps in the attic (the "victims" on whom they feed are dumped unceremoniously in the incinerator). But the machine célibataire functions here too, as the "bride" pulls victims and lovers off the street into her elevated apartment (Fig. 46), is disrobed by her male and female lovers, and then retreats to the eerie heights of the attic which is peopled by doves, more veils, and coffins containing the empty shells of those who have paid dearly for their desire (Fig. 47).

In this film the Deneuve character does not survive. At the end she dissolves into a twisting, repugnant mass of wrinkled flesh before disintegrating into a skull whose mouth is still opened in a scream. Her openly expressed desire has been fatal to her lovers, and she herself is punished for it, according to cinematic convention.

As we leave the machine age for the cybernetic age, there seems to be no answer to the despairing cry of Baron Gortz, who, on losing the box that encloses La Stilla's voice, realizes her true name: the silent one. On the other side of the conundrum, Lord Ewald wonders how Alicia can sing so well without a soul. Hadaly's machine intelligence will mimic that "soul" for him, play for him his own "preprogrammed script of the Other."[38] Edison's robot seems to typify

45. Deneuve as a vampire. (Tony Scott, *The Hunger*)

46. The "mechanical bride" on the landing of her stair. (Tony Scott, *The Hunger*)

47. The lofty feminine sphere of the "perfect woman." (Tony Scott, *The Hunger*)

not only the machines of the industrial revolution, but current artificial intelligence models of the mind as well.

The problem is that cybernetic models proceed from descriptions or intuitions about human cognitive functioning, and that all the indications are that we tend to understand ourselves in terms of how well our life patterns conform to preexisting scripts. Why should models of us be any different? Erving Goffman has described in *Frame Analysis* the way in which our everyday social interactions are aided by conventional understandings that enable us to cope with—to frame—both expected and unexpected events. These cognitive frames, he argues, affirm our beliefs in the workings of the world.[39]

Goffman's examples are fascinating and numerous and it would be unnecessary to add any more. Nevertheless, I found his views corroborated by an important example he does not mention: the "life summary," as exemplified by college reunion notes. This is a particularly fascinating instance since it suggests that people perceive their lives according to preset scripts that are imposed on them from outside. Whether or not life narratives read as a "success" story (at least for my own class), turns out to depend on a limited number of frames: job, marriage, children, and travel. Here are two typical examples (from male members of the class):

> It seems I turned out rather well—at least according to my somewhat surprised parents! Here I am, three happy kids, a lovely wife, a solid member of the depressed middle class with a fine variety of experiences since '68 . . .

> In the last five years I: finished a fellowship in nephrology; got married; took a year-long honeymoon; returned to U.S.; became a staff physician; bought a house; had a kid, stopped going out.

The irony discernible in these notes only serves to underscore the fact that the writers are conscious of the frame constraints. Those who were not conventionally successful also betray a knowledge of the frame; one member complains that he is "still, inexplicably, perhaps permanently, single;" another is at pains to explain that the "woman" slot for his success frame is now filled by his dog: "After college, I discovered how warm it feels to live with a woman. It's still true. Now I also sleep with a dog, a German short hair. That feels warm too." Some of the women commented on their inability to break out of the "success" frame: "Girlhood dreams of being a composer or stand-up comic in a nightclub have been deferred. I settle for motherhood and professordom;" "I wanted to be a country and western singer, but somehow got sidetracked into politics."[40]

These class notes showed that people not only script themselves; they set goals for their children which end up scripting the children's lives in conventional ways. None of the male children are described as "beautiful," though many of the female children are. Frames also emerged for gender roles. Only one male member of the class said that raising children was a lot of work, though many of the female members described the difficulties of mixing child care and career. None of the female members gave the impression that their husband was a possession, though a significant number of the male members listed their wives along with other material gains. A number of the men, incidentally, said that they were still looking for "the ideal woman."

There is a surprising coincidence between these "life stories" and the plot structures of fiction. Apparently, we cannot see ourselves as anything but text.[41] Roger Schank has developed computerized models of our experience that proceed along the assumption that real-world expectations function as "scripts": "Scripts are prepackaged sorts of expectations, inferences, and knowledge that are applied in common situations, like a blueprint for action without the details filled in . . . a script tells what is likely to come next in a chain of events that are stereotypes."[42] Finally, Schank also instructs his computer program in human needs and desires, developing representations that he calls "goals." From reading these class notes, one gets the feeling that Schank wouldn't have much trouble computer-generating the knowledge and belief structure of a typical Harvard graduate.

Psychoanalysis and artificial intelligence furnish endless repetitions of our self-image as coded combinations of texts, which we can understand but are at a loss to change. As Michel Serres says, "the transformational motor of our fathers has simply changed into an informational one, just as thermodynamics has changed into information theory. The conditions (of their functioning) remain those of closure, of difference, of circulation, and their end . . . is chaos, dissolution, and disorder."[43]

How, then, do we break out of the scripts that constrain us? Feminist film theory has demanded a new filmmaking practice that would either break the patriarchal models of narrative or would construct the place of the female subject differently in the processes of identification (some of these options are taken up again in the conclusion to this book). Another possibility is the creation of new readings of existing films, readings that concentrate on the subversive, rather than subservient, moments of the classical cinema. It is an ingenious strategy, and one that informs Teresa de Lauretis's exciting suggestion that certain contemporary films can be read as "remakes" of patriarchal narratives: Hitchcock's *Rebecca* remade as *Les Rendez-vous d'Anna* or *Jeanne Dielman* (Chantal Akerman), *Vertigo* remade as *Bad Timing: A Sensual Obsession* (Nicholas Roeg).[44] In a similar vein, Gertude Koch argues that feminist readings of existing films (or of star personae like Marilyn Monroe and Mae West) can come up with new interpretations.[45]

Such a strategy would regroup existing films into new textual systems, discovering new typologies and reading them against the ideologies that produced them for signs that do not fit into the system of specularity and fetishism. One thing we might look for are moments in film where the illusion fails, and the masquerade is discovered. Marcel Proust has described such a moment in the theater: "As in a transformation scene on the stage a crease in the dress of a fairy, a quivering of her tiny finger, indicate the material presence of a living actress before our eyes, whereas we were uncertain, till then, whether we were not looking merely at a projection of limelight from a lantern."[46] I take this to be the spirit of Annette Kuhn's justification for the feminist analysis of mainstream images of women: "may it not teach us to recognise inconsistencies and contradictions within dominant traditions of representation, to identify points of leverage for our own intervention: cracks and fissures through which may be captured glimpses of what might in other circumstances be possible, visions of a 'world outside the order not normally seen or thought about'?"[47]

There is such a moment in *Belle de jour*; significantly, it is the moment when Husson, the friend of the husband, comes to tell him of Séverine's double life. As Séverine waits in the hallway, she slides her hand delicately and expressively across the edge of a marble table top. The effect on the viewer is the transmission of a tactile sensation, which gains additional power because it is also an instance of "seeing with" the character. This combination of physical communication and dual narration (which comes about through the fusion of the camera-narrator and the character) is one way to break the distance and emptiness Chambers describes as being characteristic of the myth of the actress. In fact projective point-of-view shots frequently mediate a tactile experience to the viewer, a fact noted many years ago by the film theorist Siegfried Kracauer.[48] Luis Buñuel's films often communicate to the spectator on a startlingly physical level, whether by the slicing of an eye in *Un chien andalou* (someone has suggested calling this a "flinch shot")[49] or the eliciting of physical responses from the spectator through identification with characters.

There is hope from another side as well. The bachelor machines of fiction and film often dramatize a self-critical male viewpoint. This was already true in *L'Eve future*. To the grateful Lord Ewald, Edison explains that by giving Hadaly the right cues, which will always activate the identical responses on the golden records created from the best writings of poets, he will be able to replay their first meeting, immobilizing "the first (and finest) hour of love" (155). Indeed, if we never do more than recite lines at one another, why not opt for the best ones? Yet in the end, Hadaly goes down in a shipwreck that takes Alicia with it as well. Only Lord Ewald survives to meditate on his close encounter with the machine célibataire. Prophetically, Villiers predicted the end of the machine age, and correctly estimated the social pathology that finds expression in the literature, psychoanalysis, and cinema of the past hundred years.

In line with this, there is a suggestion, at the end of *Belle de jour*, that the whole series of fantasies has been, all along, the dream of the husband. As he sits in his wheelchair sleeping, an involuntary movement of his hand suggests that he is presently awakening from a dream. Suddenly, the supposedly invalid man stretches and awakens normally. This suggests that the film can be read as a male fantasy about a woman rather than as a woman's fantasy of sexuality. Buñuel, after all, was a filmmaker who started out in surrealism, where the emphasis was on the older alchemical model of union between male and female. The repeated failure of his male characters to enter into a reciprocal relationship with a woman (from his 1928 film *Un chien andalou* [*Andalusian Dog*] all the way through his last film, *Cet obscur objet de désir* [*That Obscure Object of Desire*, 1978]) leaves us with a very ambiguous message. On the one hand, the men's failure can be read as a critique of the mechanical metaphors I have been describing. On the other hand, their anxiousness speaks to the difficulty of changing inherited models of perception. But I am anticipating my conclusion.

CONCLUSION

As society changes, so do its representations; yet sometimes those representations themselves can effect change. The work of criticism can bring works to
the forum for discussion and can show how these works articulate our concerns
in unexpected ways.

Many of the films I have chosen for discussion reenact threshold moments
in the acts of perception of the societies that produced them. They dramatize
the indecision that comes before change—what I would call an experience of
liminality (from the Latin *limen*, or threshold), of being in between two spaces,
two states of mind, two systems of representation. By reenacting that uncertainty, the films often encourage the spectator to experience a change of mind.

The idea of stretching film beyond the conventional limits of cinematic language, of representation, is fundamental to the concerns I have tried to articulate throughout this volume, whose subtitle is derived from an essay by the
French author and critic Philippe Sollers. Sollers writes that "literature's goal
is not the constitution of objects, but a ciphered relation, a sliding which by
opening up different subjects outside their limits reveals objects of thought and
of the world."[1] I have tried, in the first sections of this book, to focus on films
which attempt to go beyond some of these limits. I have argued that the work
demanded of the viewer in many of these films is that of acquiring new forms
of language and representation to express new content.

Language does not necessarily bind us to what already exists if we use it in
this transformative way. Since I wrote these chapters, a few films have, in their
own way, contributed to this stretching of our cognitive horizon. Spike Lee's
Do the Right Thing moves outside of the race and class usually represented in
Hollywood films while managing to engage the sympathy and identification with
characters that typifies the entertainment cinema. His practice of cinematic
language resembles the tightly structured gags of Chaplin features (such as
Modern Times), in which the characters move in and out of the camera's field
of vision according to a theme and variation structure. The result is an unusual
blend between minute observation and a panoramic overall view of one day on
the neighborhood block—a day that brings urgent social issues to the fore. *A
World Apart*, based on Ruth First's *117 Days*, allows the spectator to experience
the agonized choices that face everyone living under apartheid. For once, a
woman protagonist, seen through the eyes of her teenage daughter, is central
to this film. In conclusion, then, I offer some thoughts for future developments
in cinema that are to be hoped for.

In the last two sections of this book, I have focused on certain problems
relating to the representation of women. We need films whose content reflects
the experience of women. It should simply be an accepted fact that women's
lives are as interesting as men's lives. In an article in *Gender Studies*, Norine
Voss has noted that women's autobiographies form a largely ignored body of

literature.[2] This situation is parallelled by the lack of filmed versions of the lives of historical women. Part of the acceptance of women as subjects of fiction will have to consist in the rediscovery of actual women's histories. As Gertrud Koch has stated, "it is this recognition of woman having her own history which is the precondition above all others for perceiving woman as subject."[3] In *A Choice of Heroes*, Mark Gerzon discusses (and shows the problems with) a panoply of male types that have served as role models for the white American male (these include, for instance, the frontiersman, the soldier, the breadwinner, the expert, and the father).[4] Films, which play such a large role in determining our role models, might offer women "a choice of heroines."

Films must allow characters of different genders full rights in the exploration of the diegetic space. Otherwise women spectators will continue to be caught in what Silvia Bovenshen has called the "transference," in which they either identify with the white masculine point of view or adopt the masochistic/ narcissistic position of identifying with whatever is defined as "other" in the film by the dominant masculine representation.[5] For instance, Judith Fetterley has coined the word "immasculation" for the woman's incorporation of the male point of view, in which "intellectually male, sexually female, one is in effect no one."[6] But this syndrome could be extended to anyone in the audience who feels left out of the group that dominates.

Neither men nor women should be limited to being two-dimensional "screen" characters. I think it important that men be offered the chance to identify with female mediators of space and narrative causality, just as women have traditionally had to identify with male ones. And just possibly, men might also enjoy films in which women are allowed to look and to return the look.[7]

Films should give a more balanced view of gender that does not do violence to the spectator's self-concept. Getting away from the stereotypical portrayal of women means, as Teresa de Lauretis has stated, that films will have to represent the differences within women as well as the differences among women. Films should not assume that all women spectators are the same, or that any given film portraying a woman character's subjectivity speaks for all women.[8]

What I have just said about the presentation of women in film applies to that of race, class, and culture as well. These will be the major issues of the 90s. We will need strong creative statements about our world if we are to understand it and understand how to change it. In some chapters I have described points of resistance to convention that could serve as guideposts to future filmmakers. Zazie's disruptive language, dual narration that lets the spectator in on the thoughts of the characters, the marking of the arranger as nonwhite and nonmale, performative space—all these are partial solutions to the need for films that operate outside of conventional norms. Remaking films while changing the sex of their protagonists (as I suggest in the case of *E.T.* and *The Wizard of Oz*) would be one way to uncover the sexual politics of familiar narratives.

The above strategies have the virtue of working within the framework of narrative film rather than denying the spectator the pleasure of following and becoming involved in a story. They may become enabling narratives that participate in the process of cognitive change in society. As Joanne Frye states in her remarkable study of women's novels, a work that problematizes narrative conventions can function "not only as cognitive instrument but also as recognitive instrument."[9] Stephen Heath makes a similar argument when he urges radical filmmakers to work "at the limits of narrative within the narrative film, at the limits of its fiction of unity."[10] This working away at the borders of intelligibility, in the space where meaning is created and not just faithfully reproduced, is central to the practice of frame-breaking as I have tried to articulate it in these pages. And, since our language reflects our reality, its transformation can help to transform our world as well.

Notes

INTRODUCTION

1. In my previous book, I explicated the relevance of frame theory to the study of surrealist texts. See *Languages of Revolt: Dada and Surrealist Literature and Film* (Durham: Duke University Press, 1983). The best summary of frame theory may be found in Mary Crawford and Roger Chaffin's "The Reader's Construction of Meaning: Cognitive Research on Gender and Comprehension," in Elizabeth A. Flynn and Patrocinio P. Schweickart, eds., *Gender and Reading* (Baltimore: The Johns Hopkins University Press, 1986), 4–10 and 26–27.

2. Benjamin Lee Whorf, *Language, Thought, and Reality* (Cambridge: MIT Press, 1984), 152.

3. Whorf, 151.

4. George Lakoff and Mark Johnson, *Metaphors We Live By* (Chicago: University of Chicago Press, 1980), 41–45.

5. André Bazin, *What is Cinema?* ed. Hugh Gray (Berkeley: University of California Press, 1967), 13–14.

1. BREAKING THE FRAME

1. Louis Malle, in an interview with Yvonne Baby, *Le Monde* 27 Oct. 1960.

2. On this point, see Gerald Prince, "Queneau et L'Anti-roman," *Neophilologus* 55 (1971): 33–40.

3. Nathalie Sarraute, *The Age of Suspicion: Essays on the Novel* (New York: George Braziller, 1963), 65–68.

4. Stephen Heath, *The Nouveau Roman* (Philadelphia: Temple University Press, 1972), 23.

5. Roland Barthes, *Essais critiques* (Paris: Seuil, 1964), 128.

6. Barthes, 131.

7. The term is from Roland Barthes, *S/Z*, trans. Richard Miller (New York: Hill & Wang, 1974).

8. The translation by Barbara Wright expertly manages to convey nearly all of these in their English equivalents: "Howcanaystinksotho" (phonetic puzzle), "Mamma couldn't stomach Papa" (spoken English), "guidenappers" (kidnappers of a tourist guide). See Raymond Queneau, *Zazie in the Metro*, trans. Barbara Wright (London: John Calder, 1982).

9. Julia Kristeva, *Semeiotikè: Recherches pour une sémanalyse* (Paris: Seuil, 1969), 151.

10. An extended discussion of the surrealists' activities and philosophy may be found in my *Languages of Revolt: Dada and Surrealist Literature and Film* (Durham: Duke University Press, 1983).

11. He complained that it lacked realism: "The film scintillated and amazed, but it lacked any real tempo, a natural respiration." Jacques Mallecot, *Louis Malle par Louis Malle* (Artigues-près-Bordeaux: Athanor, 1978), 59–60.

12. Dan Yakir, "Louis Malle: An Interview," *Film Quarterly* 31.4 (1978): 8.

13. Georges Charensol, "Qu'est-ce-qui fait courir Zazie?" *Les Nouvelles littéraires* 3 Nov. 1960: 10.

14. Louis Malle, "Zazie dans le métro," *Avant-scène du cinéma* 104 (1970): 24.

15. "Man is brought into the world by a nothing, a nothing animates him, a nothing bears him away."

16. Sigmund Freud, *The Standard Edition of the Complete Psychological Works*, trans. and ed. James Strachey, 24 vols. (London: The Hogarth Press and the Institute of Psychoanalysis, 1953–74), vol. 8, 165: "The task of dream-formation is above all to overcome the inhibition from censorship; and it is precisely this task which is solved by the displacement of psychical energy within the material of the dream-thoughts."

17. Queneau, trans. Wright, 100.

18. Louis Malle in *Le Monde*, 15.

19. André Labarthe, "Au pied de la lettre," *Cahiers du cinéma* 114 (1960): 58–60.

20. François Mars, "L'autopsie du gag, 2" *Cahiers du cinéma* 116 (1961): 29. See his book *Le Gag* (Paris: Cerf, 1964).

21. Barthes, *Essais*, 127.

22. Christian Metz, *Langage et cinéma*, (Paris: Larousse, 1971), 132.

2. FILM WRITING AND THE POETICS OF SILENCE

1. Stanley Cavell, *The World Viewed* (Cambridge: Harvard University Press, 1971), 14.

2. Bazin, "On the *politique des auteurs*," in Jim Hillier, ed., *Cahiers du Cinéma. The 1950's: Neo-realism, Hollywood, New Wave* (Cambridge: Harvard University Press, 1985), 248–59.

3. Jean-Pierre Vernant, *Les Origines de la pensée grecque*, 4th ed. ([1962] Paris: Presses Universitaires de France, 1981).

4. My comments on the Greek texts were prepared with the assistance of Haun Saussy, who was my research assistant at Duke University.

5. Georg Wilhelm Friedrich Hegel, *The Philosophy of History*, trans. J. Sibree ([1899] New York: Dover, 1956), 220. I have corrected the translation.

6. Sophocles, *Oedipus Tyrannus*, ed. A. C. Pearson (Oxford: Oxford University Press, 1985), line 25 of the commentary. The commentary by Aristophanes the Grammarian, reprinted in all the standard Oxford editions of the play in Greek, is not translated in any English language text that I have found.

7. See Derrida's discussion of Foucault's *Histoire de la folie* in *Writing and Difference*, trans. Alan Bass (Chicago: University of Chicago Press, 1978), 40: "either . . . The Socratic moment and its entire posterity immediately partake in the Greek logos that has no contrary . . . or . . . the Socratic moment and the victory over the Caliclesian hybris already are the marks of a deportation and an exile of logos from itself, the wounds left within it by a decision, a difference; and then the structure of exclusion that Foucault wishes to describe in his book could not have been born with classical reason. It would have to have been consummated and reassured and smoothed over throughout all the centuries of philosophy."

8. Jean Anouilh, *Antigone and Eurydice: Two Plays* (London: Methuen, 1951), 93: "Rien n'est vrai que ce qu'on ne dit pas."

9. The characters' consciousness of role playing is foregrounded by Anouilh. For instance Creon says he has the bad role, Antigone the good one. Anouilh, 76.

10. Alain Robbe-Grillet, *The Erasers*, trans. Richard Howard (New York: Grove Press, 1964).

11. See the analysis by Bruce Morissette in *The Novels of Robbe-Grillet* (Ithaca: Cornell University Press, 1975).

12. Claudio Guillén, *Literature as System: Essays toward the Theory of Literary History* (Princeton: Princeton University Press, 1971), 13.

13. Nathalie Sarraute, *The Age of Suspicion: Essays on the Novel*, trans. Maria Jolles (New York: Braziller, 1963).

14. Stanley Cavell, "Ending the Waiting Game: A Reading of Beckett's *Endgame*," in *Must We Mean What We say?* ([1969] Cambridge: Cambridge University Press, 1976), 126.

15. Cavell, 156.

16. Cavell, 155.

17. Cavell, 149.

18. Miriam Hansen, "Traces of Transgression in *Apocalypse Now*," *Social Text* 3 (1980): 128.

19. See Hansen, 126.

20. Cavell, 160.

21. Cavell, 148–49.

3. FORMS OF REPRESENTATION IN *LA NUIT DE VARENNES*

1. "All the interior lines of the painting, and above all those that come from the central reflection, point towards the very thing that is represented, but absent . . . in Classical thought, the personage for whom the representation exists, and who represents himself within it, recognizing himself therein as an image or reflection, he who ties together all the interlacing threads of the 'representation in the form of a picture or table'—he is never to be found in the table himself." Michel Foucault, *The Order of Things: An Archeology of the Human Sciences* (New York: Vintage Books, 1973), 308.

2. "From the right, there streams in through an invisible window the pure volume of a light that renders all representation visible . . . we are observing ourselves being observed by the painter, and made visible to his eyes by the same light that enables us to see him." Foucault, 6.

3. Marie-Claire Ropars-Wuilleumier, *Le Texte divisé: Essai sur l'écriture filmique* (Paris: Presses Universitaires de France, 1981), 143–59.

4. Of course Scola is anticipating history, since he conveys, in the eighteenth century, a nostalgia for a form of storytelling that did not reach its apogee until the nineteenth. But then Roland Barthes has argued (persuasively, I think) that the mode of storytelling we call nineteenth century realism from the beginning conveyed a "nostalgic reality." See Roland Barthes, *The Grain of the Voice: Interviews 1962–1980*, trans. Linda Coverdale (New York: Hill & Wang, 1985), 4.

5. Ross Chambers, *Story and Situation: Narrative Seduction and the Power of Fiction* (Minnesota: University of Minnesota Press, 1984).

6. Since writing this I have had the opportunity of reading Elena Gascon-Vera's typescript, "Giacomo Casonova and the Enlightenment of Women in the 18th Century," which concurs with this view.

7. In his disarming memoirs, Casanova explains that even his famous wit is falsely ascribed to him; in Paris, he explains, his most celebrated rejoinders come from his insufficient knowledge of the language. Thus, when Madame de Pompadour makes a remark at the opera about a singer's ugly legs, he unwittingly answers: "Whenever I examine the beauty of a woman, *la première chose que j'écarte, ce sont les jambes*." Giacomo Casanova, *The Life and Memoirs of Casanova*, trans. Arthur Machen ([1929] New York: Da Capo, 1984), 250. The translator evidently found this witticism as untranslatable as I do (*écarter* in this context means both to set aside and to spread apart). Casanova's disingenuousness is similar to that of the classical text: he conceals his artifice the better to seduce.

8. It may be significant that Casanova nods off in the stagecoach while trying to explain to the three women the most important element of love. The medium closeup

shot that frames him is the only one that may be said to quote Alexandre Volkoff's 1927 film *Casanova*; in Volkoff's film that shot shows the hero in the bloom of manhood setting out for Russia in pursuit of a Venetian noblewoman.

9. Chambers, 51.

10. Moncure Daniel Conway, *The Life of Thomas Paine* (Folcroft, Pa.: Folcroft Library Editions, 1974), 126.

11. From the manifesto: "What kind of office must that be in a government which requires for its execution neither experience nor ability? That may be abandoned to the desperate chance of birth, that may be filled by an idiot, a madman, a tyrant, with equal effect as by the good, the virtuous, and the wise?" Conway, 126.

12. Foucault, 304.

13. Hayden White, *Metahistory: The Historical Imagination in Nineteenth-Century Europe* (Baltimore and London: The Johns Hopkins University Press, 1973), 15–16.

14. Chambers, 13: "If readability (or interpretability) is the power literary texts have of producing meanings, a power achieved by virtue of the reification of literary discourse into ' text,' then seduction is the inevitable means by which the alienated text achieves value by realizing its potential of readability. However, if this readerly quality of text is a function of textual alienation, then we need not be surprised to discover . . . that textual seductiveness relies in growing measure on techniques and conceptions of art that today we associate rather with the notion of the ' writerly.' "

15. Nicholas Edmé Restif de la Bretonne, *Les Nuits de Paris ou le spectateur nocturne*, 16 parts in 8 vols. (Paris: chez Merigot jeune, libraire, 1791–94), vol. 8, part 16, 292–97 and 306–308.

16. Restif de la Bretonne, 424–25.

17. Lucien Dällenbach, *Le récit speculaire. Essai sur la mise en abyme* (Paris: Seuil, 1977), 21.

4. TRUFFAUT AND COCTEAU

1. Jean Cocteau, *Orphée*, ed. E. Freeman (London: Blackwell, 1976), 103.

2. Maurice Blanchot, *The Space of Literature* (Lincoln: University of Nebraska Press, 1982), 174: "Orpheus's gaze is Orpheus's ultimate gift to the work. It is a gift whereby he refuses, whereby he sacrifices the work, bearing himself toward the origin according to desire's measureless movement."

3 . François Truffaut, *La Chambre verte*, in *L'Avant-scène du cinéma* 215 (1978): 41.

4. Roland Barthes, *Camera Lucida*, trans. Richard Howard (New York: Hill and Wang, 1981), 73.

5. Walter Benjamin, "Eine Kleine Geschichte der Photographie" [1931], in *Gesammelte Schriften*, 6 vols. (Frankfurt am Main: Suhrkamp, 1977), vol. 2, 368–85.

6. Siegfried Kracauer, *Das Ornament der Masse* (Frankfurt am Main: Suhrkamp, 1963), 26.

7. Kracauer, 26.

8. Kracauer, 32.

9. André Bazin, *Le Cinéma de l'occupation et de la résistance* (Paris, 1975), 20–21.

10. See Annette Insdorf, *François Truffaut* (Boston: Twayne Publishers, 1978).

11. The story, along with an excellent translation and notes by Eugene P. Walz, appears in *Mosaic* 16.1–2 (1983): 125–43.

12. François Truffaut, "A Certain Tendency of the French Cinema," in Bill Nichols, ed., *Movies and Methods*, 2 vols. (Berkeley: University of California Press, 1976), vol. 1, 234–35.

13. E. R. Dodds, *The Greeks and the Irrational* (Berkeley: University of California Press, 1968), 154.

14. François Truffaut, *The Films in My Life*, trans. Leonard Mayhew (New York: Simon and Schuster, 1978), 6.

15. Terrence Rafferty, "Reflections" *The New Yorker* (31 Dec. 1984), 39.

16. Bloom writes that "every poet begins (however "unconsciously") by rebelling more strongly against the consciousness of death's necessity than all other men and women do." *The Anxiety of Influence* (New York: Oxford University Press, 1975), 10.

17. Bloom, 15–16.

18. Bloom, 147.

19. Bloom, 15: "The later poet . . . yields up part of his own human and imaginative endowment, so as to separate himself from others, including the precursor, and he does this in his poem by so stationing it in regard to the parent-poem as to make that poem undergo an *askesis* too; the precursor's endowment is also truncated."

20. Italo Calvino, *Invisible Cities*, trans. William Weaver ([1972] New York: Harcourt Brace Jovanovich, 1974), 109–10.

21. As a matter of fact de Chirico, whose "surrealist" paintings were done ten years before the movement was founded, was what Breton would later call a "surrealist in spite of himself."

22. To continue the mise-en-abyme of these intertextual citations, it is probable that my own juxtaposition of Cocteau and de Chirico comes from reading Wallace Fowlie's description of Cocteau's work: "His personal genius is like the surrealist genius of Giorgio de Chirico, who in his paintings creates a magical world where a Greek temple may cohabit with a glass-covered wardrobe, where a perspective and *trompe-l'oeil* convert a familiar world into a mystery." Wallace Fowlie, *Age of Surrealism* (1950; Bloomington: Indiana University Press, 1960), 123.

23. Stephen Heath, *Questions of Cinema* (Bloomington: Indiana University Press, 1981), 114.

24. As Chris Marker has brilliantly shown in his film *La Jetée*, that image is one that evokes our own death.

25. Peter Brooks, *Reading for the Plot* (1984; New York: Random House, 1985), 96–112.

26. Brooks, 103.

27. André Bazin, *What is Cinema?* (Berkeley and Los Angeles: University of California Press, 1967), 17–22.

5. MEDIATED VISION

1. In *Narration in Light: Studies in Cinematic Point of View* (Baltimore: The Johns Hopkins University Press, 1986), George M. Wilson argues against interpreting the second shot subjectively, saying that "[Lisa] is now merely the subject of *our* perception and is utterly removed from the perspective that earlier she had held" (103–104). Our disagreement points to the fact that the subtle art of dual narration is quite often a matter of interpretation. Elsewhere (87–88) the writer comes close to describing something like dual narration in his treatment of "reflected subjectivity." Here, though, his typology is unable to distinguish between effects of mise-en-scène (attributable to the arranger) and effects of the camera narrator. Seymour Chatman touches briefly on dual narration when he describes the "odd phenomenon" of "a character who is both object and mediator of our vision." See his *Story and Discourse* (Ithaca: Cornell University Press, 1978), 160.

2. Paul Hernadi, "Dual Perspective in Prose Fiction," *Comparative Literature* 25 (1972): 32–43.

3. Tania Modleski has argued persuasively that the narrative of *Letter from an Unknown Woman* still revolves largely around the male character whose reading of the letter frames the woman's story. See her essay "Time and Desire in the Woman's Film,"

Cinema Journal 23.3 (1984): 19–30. My analysis of dual narration in this text is an attempt to provide an answer to her questions, "How are we to begin attempting to locate a feminine voice in texts which repress it and which, as . . . in *Letter from an Unknown Woman*, grant possession of the Word only to men?" (22).

4. The term "arranger" was first proposed by David Hayman to describe the controlling consciousness of *Ulysses*, a text so polyphonic as to be decentered in its narrative point of view. See David Hayman, *Ulysses: the Mechanics of Meaning* (Englewood Cliffs, N.J.: Prentice-Hall, 1970), 70: "I use the term 'arranger' to designate a figure who can be identified neither with the author nor with his narrators, but who exercises an increasing degree of overt control over his increasingly challenging materials."

5. George Bluestone, *Novels into Film* (Baltimore: The Johns Hopkins University Press, 1957), 336.

6. Christian Metz, "Current Problems in Film Theory: Christian Metz on Jean Mitry's *L'Esthétique et pyschologie du cinéma, II*," *Screen* 14.1–2 (1973): 69.

7. Siegfried Kracauer, *Theory of Film* (New York: Oxford University Press, 1965), 232–44.

8. Alain Robbe-Grillet, "Notes sur la localisation et les déplacements du point de vue dans la description romanesque," *Revue des lettres modernes* 5.36–38 (1958): 257.

9. Tzvetan Todorov, "Les Catégories du récit littéraire," *Communications* 8 (1966): 141–43.

10. Malcolm Lowry, *Under the Volcano* ([1947] Philadelphia: J. B. Lippincott, 1965), 14.

11. I take my description of the classical Hollywood narrative from David Bordwell, *Narration in the Fiction Film* (Madison: University of Wisconsin Press, 1985). See especially pages 156–204.

12. Nick Browne, "The Spectator-in-the-Text: The Rhetoric of *Stagecoach*," in *The Rhetoric of Filmic Narration* (Ann Arbor: UMI Research Press, 1982), 12.

13. Bordwell, 231: "Through an emphasis on 'character,' the cinema could now achieve the seriousness of contemporary literature and drama, insofar as the latter were thought to portray modern man's confrontation with a mysterious cosmos."

14. Luis Buñuel, *Tristana* (script) in *Avant-scène du cinéma* 110 (1971).

15. See John Berger, *Ways of Seeing* (New York: Penguin, 1972), 54: "In the average European oil painting of the nude the principal protagonist is never painted. He is the spectator in front of the picture and he is presumed to be a man. Everything is addressed to him. Everything must appear to be the result of his being there. It is for him that the figures have assumed their nudity."

16. Bal argues that the narrator, being "that agent which utters the linguistic signs which constitute the text," is impersonal. See Mieke Bal, *Narratology* (Toronto: University of Toronto Press, 1985), 120.

17. Berger, 47. See also Laura Mulvey, "Visual Pleasure and Narrative Cinema," in Karyn Kay and Gerald Peary, eds., *Women and the Cinema* (New York: E. P. Dutton, 1977), 412–28.

18. For an analysis of this "duplicitous narrative," see Kristin Thompson, "The Duplicitous Text: An Analysis of 'Stage Fright,' " *Film Reader* 2 (1977): 52–64.

19. Marie-Claire Ropars-Wuilleumier, *De la littérature au cinéma; genèse d'une écriture* (Paris: A. Colin, 1970), 131–32.

6. WOMEN AND FILM SPACE

1. Claudine Hermann, *Les Voleuses de langue* (Paris: Editions des femmes, 1976), 150.

2. I agree with Bruce Kawin's view, presented in *Mindscreen: Bergman, Godard, and First Person Film* (Princeton University Press, 1978), that "*Persona* is about film—

its 'own' . . . awareness of being a film and Bergman's awareness that he is making a film—as much as it is about the relationship between Alma and Elizabeth" (105–106). Similarly Susan Sontag states that "in *Persona* it is precisely language . . . which is in question." See *"Persona:* The Film in Depth," in Leo Braudy and Morris Dickstein, eds., *Great Film Directors* (New York: Oxford, 1978), 84. Kawin argues (127) that the boy in the prologue represents the artist, an opinion echoed by Frank Gado in *The Films of Ingmar Bergman* (Durham: Duke University Press, 1986), 326.

3. Antonin Artaud, *The Theatre and Its Double* (New York: Grove Press, 1958), 92.

4. Birgitta Steene argues against using feminist criteria in evaluating Bergman's treatment of women, since he seeks to "create his own subjective landscape . . . and to project, through his women characters, his own personal *mythos.*" See "Bergman's Portrait of Women: Sexism or Suggestive Metaphor?" in Patricia Erens, ed., *Sexual Strategems: The World of Women in Film* (New York: Horizon Press, 1972), 96. I think it is important, nevertheless, to signal the presence of gender stereotypes no matter what the artist's alibi for using them.

5. Here I should signal two recent readings of *Persona,* which, though different from the one offered here, are in agreement with me on this point. P. Adams Sitney has suggested a reading whereby Alma is the patient and Elizabeth the silent analyst. This pair in turn is the fantasy of the male adult subject, fictively represented as a child or adolescent by Elizabeth's son and by the young boy of the prologue. The film would be Bergman's expression of his "fear of psychoanalysis as a threat to creativity." See P. Adams Sitney, "The Analytic Text: A Reading of *Persona," October* 38 (1986): 113–30. Lucy Fischer considers that the cinematic apparatus itself functions as the object of desire in the film: *"Persona* is not only a film that, on a dramatic level, sees woman as mother, and mother as quintessential actress, but one that creates an image to literalize the Oedipal perspective on narrative and associate woman's body with the cinematic apparatus." Lucy Fischer, *Shot/Countershot: Film Tradition and Women's Cinema* (Princeton University Press, 1989), 80.

6. David Bordwell and Kristin Thompson, *Film Art,* 2nd ed. (New York: Alfred A. Knopf, 1986), 94–95.

7. Edward Branigan, *Point of View in the Cinema* (The Hague: Mouton, 1985), 123.

8. Previous writing on this film has focused on the relationship between the main protagonist and her roommate, who moves out to get married (the "girlfriends" of the title). See Annette Kuhn, *Women's Pictures: Feminism and the Cinema* (London: Routledge and Kegan Paul, 1982); Rebecca A. Bailin, *"Girlfriends:* No Celebration of Female Bonding," *Jump Cut* 20 (May 1979): 3; and Lucy Fischer, *Shot/Countershot,* 232–49.

9. Fischer, 242.

10. Stephen Heath, "Questions of Property: Film and Nationhood," *Ciné-Tracts* 1.4 (1978): 3.

11. Stephen Heath, *Questions of Cinema* (Bloomington: Indiana University Press, 1981), 64: "The narrative space of film is today not simply a theoretical and practical actuality but is a crucial and political avant-garde problem. . . . a politically consequent materialism in film is not to be expressed as veering contact past internal content in order to proceed with 'film and film' but rather as a work on the constructions and relations of meaning and subject in a specific signifying practice in a given socio-historical situation."

12. Since developing this concept I have come across Tania Modleski's concurrent view that feminist criticism as a whole can be seen as "performative." See Tania Modleski, "Some Functions of Feminist Criticism, of the Scandal of the Mute Body," *October* 49 (1989): 3–24.

13. E. Ann Kaplan, *Women and Film: Both Sides of the Camera* (New York: Methuen, 1983), 96.

14. See Mary Ann Doane, "The Voice in the Cinema: The Articulation of Body and Space," *Yale French Studies* 60 (1980): 33–50: "The value of thinking the deployment

of the voice in the cinema by means of its relation to the body (that of the character; that of the spectator) lies in an understanding of the cinema . . . as a series of spaces including that of the spectator. . . . Whatever the arrangement of interpenetration of the various spaces, they constitute a place where signification intrudes. The various techniques and strategies for the deployment of the voice contribute heavily to the definition of the form that 'place' takes" (50).

15. Peter Handke, *The Left-Handed Woman*, trans. Ralph Manheim (New York: Farrar, Straus and Giroux, 1978), 40.

16. See E. Ann Kaplan, 99.

17. Tania Modleski, *October* 49 (Summer 1989): 18.

7. SCRIPTING CHILDREN'S MINDS

1. Sigmund Freud, *Beyond the Pleasure Principle* (1920) in *The Standard Edition of the Complete Psychological Works*, trans. and ed. James Strachey, 24 vols. (London: The Hogarth Press and the Institute of Psychoanalysis, 1953–74), vol. 18, 1–64.

2. Jean Piaget, *Play, Dreams and Imitation in Childhood* (New York: W. W. Norton, 1962), 169ff.

3. I am using the definition by André Jolles, according to whom a myth is the attempt to answer a question: "When the universe is created unto man by *question* and *answer*, a *form* arises, which we will call myth." See his *Formes simples* (Paris: Seuil, 1972), 77–101. This is a translation of the 1930 German edition *Einfache Formen*.

4. Christian Metz, *The Imaginary Signifier*, trans. Celia Britton et al. (Bloomington: Indiana University Press, 1982), 58–63.

5. Peter Brooks, *Reading for the Plot: Design and Intention in Narrative* (New York: Vintage Books, 1984): "As well as having form, plots must generate force: the force that makes the connection of incidents powerful, that shapes the confused material of a life into an intentional structure that in turn generates new insights about how life can be told" (282–83).

6. Piaget, 172.

7. Lawrence Kohlberg, "The Young Child as a Philosopher," in *Child Psychology and Childhood Education*, ed. Lawrence Kohlberg (New York and London: Longman, 1987), 17.

8. Donald P. Spence, *Narrative Truth and Historical Truth: Meaning and Interpretation in Psychoanalysis* (New York: W. W. Norton, 1982).

9. Roger C. Schank and Robert P. Abelson, *Scripts, Plans, Goals and Understanding* (Hillsdale, N.J.: Lawrence Erlbaum Assoc., 1977).

10. Michael Patrick Hearn, ed., *The Wizard of Oz: The Screenplay* (New York: Bantam Doubleday Dell, 1989), 128.

11. Melanie Klein, *The Psychoanalysis of Children*, trans. Alix Strachey ([1932] New York: Delacorte Press/S. Lawrence, 1975), 153; and *Contributions to Psychoanalysis 1921–1945* (London: The Hogarth Press, 1948), 212: "From the early identification with the mother in which the anal-sadistic level so largely preponderates, the little girl derives jealousy and hatred and forms a cruel super-ego after the maternal imago. . . . But the more the identification with the mother becomes stablized on a genital basis, the more it will be characterized by the devoted kindness of a bountiful mother-ideal." See also 220n: "In both sexes the turning away from the mother as an oral love-object results from the oral frustrations undergone through her . . . the mother who frustrates persists in the child's life as the mother who is feared."

12. This thought is not absent from the consciousness of boys; Klein even relates the dream of a boy in which the negative mother-imago appears as a witch (Klein, *Psychoanalysis of Children*, 56). But the identification with the father makes for less of a traumatic separation, so that the negative mother image is less severe.

13. In the *Introductory Lectures on Psychoanalysis*, Freud has described a patient's dream in which going to the theater stands as a metaphor for getting married (Freud, vol. 16, 225). Dorothy's loss of innocence as she sees "behind the scenes" must be swiftly covered up.

14. There are two competent psychoanalytic essays on the film. In Harvey Greenberg's essay, the film is seen as an emblem of Dorothy's rite of passage, "the death of her child self and the rebirth of a newer, lovelier Dorothy." *The Movies on Your Mind* (New York: Dutton, 1975), 30. Daniel Dervin, who describes the film as a journey through various phallic symbols (the tornado, the skyline of Oz, the organ the wizard plays, the witch's broomstick, and the film image) and breast symbols (all the screens, including the crystal balls, the window of the house in the tornado, and the film screen) problematizes Dorothy's position somewhat by allowing that the message is "not very liberated." *Through a Freudian Lens Deeply. A Psychoanalysis of Cinema* (Lawrence Erlbaum: Analytic Press, 1975), 63.

15. Melanie Klein, "Some Reflections on the Oresteia," in *Our Adult World and Other Essays* (New York: Basic Books, 1963), 51.

16. In the *Introductory Lectures on Psychoanalysis*, Freud uses the term "coquetry" in describing the little girl's attempt to seduce the father: "An affectionate attachment to her father, a need to get rid of her mother as superfluous and to take her place, a coquetry which already employs the methods of later womanhood—these offer a charming picture, especially in small girls, which makes us forget the possibly grave consequences lying behind this infantile situation." Freud, vol. 16, 333.

17. Several women have written convincingly on the masquerade as a defense. Joan Rivière states that "to masquerade is to manufacture a lack in the form of a certain distance between oneself and one's image." See "Womanliness as Masquerade," in Hendrik M. Ruitenbeek, ed., *Psychoanalysis and Female Sexuality* (New Haven: College and University Press, 1966), 82. In Luce Irigaray's *This Sex Which is Not One* (Ithaca: Cornell University Press, 1985), the masquerade is described as "an alienated or false version of femininity arising from the woman's awareness of the man's desire for her to be his other . . . the masquerade permits woman to experience desire not in her own right but as the man's desire situates her." (Publisher's note on selected terms, 220). Mary Ann Doane explains that "the very fact that we can speak of a woman 'using' her sex or 'using' her body for particular gains is highly significant—it is not that a man cannot use his body in this way but that he doesn't have to." See "Film and the Masquerade: Theorising the Female Spectator," *Screen* 23.3–4 (1982): 82. Freud also states that the physical vanity of women is due to the circumstance that "they are bound to value their charms more highly as a late compensation for sexual inferiority." See Freud, vol. 22, 132.

18. For an analysis of Baum's *The Wizard of Oz* as a political allegory see Henry M. Littlefield, "*The Wizard of Oz*: Parable on Populism," *American Quarterly* 16.1 (1964): 47–58.

19. *New York Times*, 28 July 1986, natl. ed.: A10; 25 Oct. 1986, natl. ed.:A1; and 26 Oct. 1986, natl. ed.: A30.

20. There is no doubt that Freud held a gloomy view of the relations between men and women. Women identify with their mothers and thus become attractive to men whose Oedipus attachment to their own mother is transferred onto them; but a woman really loves only her child, who represents the penis she lacks. Freud concludes that "a man's love and a woman's are a phase apart psychologically." See the essay on "Femininity," Freud, vol. 22, 134.

21. Jeffrey Drezner, "*E.T.*: An Odyssey of Loss," *Psychoanalytic Review* 70.2 (1983): 272.

22. Kohlberg, 36.

23. As Umberto Eco has pointed out, the quotation is a complicated one which only an adult and visually literate filmgoer, perhaps, can fully appreciate: "Nobody can enjoy

the scene if he does not share, at least, the following elements of intertextual competence: (1) he must know where the second character comes from (Spielberg citing Lucas); (2) he must know something about the links among the two directors; (3) he must know that both monsters have been designed by Rambaldi and that, consequently, they are linked by some form of brotherhood." See Umberto Eco, *Travels in Hyperreality* (San Diego: Harcourt Brace Jovanovich, 1986), 197–211.

24. I take my observations on romanticism from the following: Marthe Robert, *Origins of the Novel*, trans. Sacha Rabinovitch ([1972] Bloomington, Ind.: Indiana University Press, 1980), 64–80; and René Wellek, *Concepts of Criticism* (New Haven: Yale University Press, 1963), 128–98.

25. Marthe Robert on the romantic hero as foundling: "As always, he rewrites his life in paradise because he finds life on earth unendurable; as always, he compensates for his humble condition by constructing an ideal kingdom out of nothing; and as always, he believes what he wants to believe and, thanks to his all-powerful imagination, proves the world's inadequacy" (65).

26. Freud, vol. 18, 65–144 ("Group Psychology and the Analysis of the Ego") and vol. 19, 1–59 ("The Ego and the Id").

27. On this topic, see Edgar Morin, *Les Stars* (Paris: Seuil, 1972).

28. Metz, 61.

8. THE MYTH OF THE PERFECT WOMAN

1. *New York Times*, I:3, 20 Oct. 1985.

2. Michel Serres, "C'était avant l'exposition (universelle)," in Harald Szeemann, ed., *Junggesellenmaschinen/Machines Célibataires* (Venice: Alfieri, 1975), 68–69.

3. André Bazin, "The Myth of Total Cinema," in *What Is Cinema*, trans. Hugh Gray, 2 vols. (Berkeley: University of California Press, 1967 and 1971), vol. 1, 17–22.

4. Evelyn Fox Keller, *Reflections on Gender and Science* (New Haven: Yale University Press, 1985), 53–61.

5. Michel Carrouges, *Les machines célibataires* (Paris: Chêne, 1976), 24: "Le mythe des machines célibataires signifie de façon évidente l'empire simultané du machinisme et du monde de la terreur."

6. To some extent, Marx's mechanistic model can be blamed for his failure to anticipate that the first socialist revolution would occur in Russia, rather than in the industrialized European nations. See Paul Sweezy, "The Communist Manifesto after 100 Years," in *The Present as History* (New York: Monthly Review Press, 1953), 3–29.

7. Albert Cook has written the best account of the sexual mechanics of Duchamp's *La Mariée...* and their import for modernity. See Albert Cook, "Marcel Duchamp's Modification of Surrealism," *Stanford Literature Review* 9 (1985): 127–45. A portion of Duchamp's notes may be found in Lucy Lippard, ed., *Dadas on Art* (Englewood Cliffs, N.J.: Prentice-Hall, 1971).

8. Cook, 129.

9. Cook, 136.

10. This is especially the case for *L'Eve future*. See Edgar Morin, *Le Cinéma ou l'homme imaginaire* (Paris: Minuit, 1956), 50; André Bazin, 25; Annette Michelson, "On the Eve of the Future: The Reasonable Facsimile and the Philosophical Toy," *October* 28 (1984): 3–20; and Raymond Bellour, "Ideal Hadaly," *Camera Obscura* 15 (1986): 112–34. Of the Jules Verne text, Michel Carrouges says that it has "nothing to do with an anticipation of cinema." See Michel Carrouges, "Mode d'emploi" in *Les Machines célibataires* (Venice: Alfieri, 1975), 36. I will be arguing that Verne's fiction anticipates aspects of film spectatorship; Carrouges's remarks are directed at the cinematic apparatus.

11. Villiers de l'Isle Adam, *Eve of the Future Eden*, trans. Marilyn Gaddis Rose (Lawrence, Kansas: Coronado Press, 1981).

12. A. M. Turing, "Computing Machinery and Intelligence," *Mind* 59 (1950): 433–60.

13. Villiers, 227.

14. We should not forget that Edison devised his prototype as a means of saving men from the rapaciousness of real women who masquerade themselves in order to prey on respectable men ("The man whose passions they arouse is a prey given up to every kind of enslavement. The women are fatally, blindly obeying an obscure satiation principle of their malign essence," 127).

15. Ross Chambers, "L'Ange et l'automate; variations sur le mythe de l'actrice de Nerval à Proust," *Archives des lettres modernes* 128 (1971): 3–80.

16. Villiers, 183–4.

17. Sigmund Freud, *The Standard Edition of the Complete Psychological Works*, trans. and ed. James Strachey, 24 vols. (London: The Hogarth Press and the Institute of Psychoanalysis, 1953–74), vol. 11, 198. For a thorough analysis of Freud's writings on women, see Sarah Kofman, *The Enigma of Woman: Woman in Freud's Writings*, trans. Catherine Porter (Ithaca: Cornell University Press, 1985).

18. Excellent discussions of Freud's view of the feminine are to be found in Mary Ann Doane, "Film and the Masquerade: Theorising the Female Spectator," *Screen* 23.3–4 (1982): 74–87; and Sarah Kofman, "Freud's 'Rhapsodic Supplement' on Femininity," *Discourse* 4 (1981–82): 37–73. See also Joan Riviere, "Womanliness as Masquerade" in Hendrik M. Ruitenbeek, *Psychoanalysis and Female Sexuality* (New Haven: College and University Press, 1966), 209–20.

19. "Faire de l'actrice notre 'Muse' c'est . . . nous déclarer distancés d'une culture où nous ne voyons plus qu'un univers de signes, que nous *regardons* par conséquent au lieu de la *vivre*." Chambers, 21.

20. "L'assomption jubilatoire de son image spéculaire par l'être encore plongé dans l'impuissance motrice et la dépendance du nourrissage qu'est le petit homme à ce stade *infans*, nous paraîtra dès lors manifester en une situation exemplaire la matrice symbolique ou le *je* se précipite en une forme primordiale." Jacques Lacan, "Le stade du miroir comme formateur de la fonction du Je," *Ecrits* I (Paris: Editions du Seuil, 1966), 90. The translation by Alan Sheridan does not make clear Lacan's insistence on the male gendered child. See Jacques Lacan, *Ecrits: A Selection*, trans. Alan Sheridan (New York: W. W. Norton, 1977), 2.

21. A discussion which I find particularly helpful is Stephen Heath's "Difference," *Screen* 19.3 (Autumn 1978): 50–112. For a more extensive treatment by film theorists of Lacanian psychology, see Bill Nichols, *Ideology and the Image* (Bloomington: Indiana University Press, 1981), 30–34, and Kaja Silverman, *The Subject of Semiotics* (New York: Oxford University Press, 1983), 149–93.

22. Roland Barthes, *Mythologies*, trans. Annette Lavers ([1972] New York: Hill and Wang, 1986), 56. I have slightly changed the translation where clarification was needed.

23. Chambers, 10.

24. See the essay "Living Dolls and 'Real Women' " by Frances Borzello, Annette Kuhn, Jill Pack, and Cassandra Wedd in Annette Kuhn, *The Power of the Image* (London: Routledge and Kegan Paul, 1985), 9–18.

25. Harald Szeeman, "Les Machines célibataires," in *Les Machines célibataires*, 10.

26. "Now, for the first time, Nathanael caught sight of Olympia's beautifully formed face. Only her eyes appeared to him curiously fixed and dead. But as he stared more and more intently through the glasses it seemed as though humid moonbeams were beginning to shine in Olympia's eyes. It was as though the power of sight were only now awakening, the flame of life flickering more and more brightly." E. T. A. Hoffman, *The Tales of Hoffman*, trans. Michael Bullock (New York: Frederick Ungar Publishing Co., 1963), 21.

27. I am greatly indebted to Professor Stanley Cavell for these remarks on *The Sand-*

man. He has pointed out how, in the Hollywood melodrama, woman is born of the man's look. For instance, in *Blonde Venus*, it is the man's look which marks the beginning of the heroine's story as a woman.

28. "A single look from her heavenly eyes expresses more than any earthly language," Hoffman, 28. Nathanael experiences the ecstasy of communion with self.

29. Enno Patalas, "Metropolis, Scene 103," trans. Miriam Hansen, *Camera Obscura* 15 (1986): 171.

30. Freud, vol. 21, 147–58.

31. Christian Metz, "Photography and Fetish," *October* 34 (1985): 87–88.

32. Bazin vol. 1, 15.

33. Readers familiar with feminist film theory will realize that in discussing fetishism and sadism I take my inspiration from Laura Mulvey's essay, "Visual Pleasure and Narrative Cinema," *Screen* 16.3 (Autumn 1975): 6–18.

34. Heath, "Difference," 92.

35. Miriam Hansen, "Pleasure, Ambivalence, Identification: Valentino and Female Spectatorship," *Cinema Journal* 25: 4 (1986), 11.

36. Linda Williams, "When the Woman Looks" in Mary Ann Doane, et al., ed., *Re-Vision* (Frederick, Maryland: University Publications of America, 1984), 83–99.

37. Mary Ann Doane, "The 'Woman's Film': Possession and Address," in *Re-Vision* 70. See also Mary Ann Doane, "The Clinical Eye: Medical Discourses in the 'Women's Film' of the 1940's," in Susan Rubin Suleiman, ed., *The Female Body in Western Culture: Contemporary Perspectives* (Cambridge: Harvard University Press, 1986), 152–74.

38. This particularly apt expression is one that Professor Stanley Cavell used in his graduate seminar in philosophy at Harvard University in 1985. I am greatly indebted to Mr. Cavell and to the other members of the seminar for the opportunity to discuss some of the ideas presented here.

39. Erving Goffman, *Frame Analysis: An Essay on the Organization of Experience* (Cambridge: Harvard University Press, 1974), 14–15.

40. *Harvard and Radcliffe College Class of 1968; Fifteenth Anniversary Report* (Ward Hill, Mass.: DBL Company, 1983), passim.

41. Umberto Eco tries to distinguish between "common frames" related to real world experiences and "intertextual frames" derived from previous experiences with texts. The common frame of a train robbery would differ, he argues, from the intertextual frame established in films (Umberto Eco, *The Role of the Reader* [Bloomington: Indiana University Press, 1979], 21–22). But in fact, this amounts to what Jerome Bruner calls the "naive realist" position—the assumption that there is anything primary about "real" experience. See Jerome Bruner, *Actual Minds, Possible Worlds* (Cambridge: Harvard University Press, 1986), 98, and Nelson Goodman, *Of Mind and Other Matters* (Cambridge: Harvard University Press, 1984), 37ff.

42. Roger C. Schank, *The Cognitive Computer: On Language, Learning, and Artificial Intelligence* (Reading, Mass.: Addison-Wesley Publishing Company, 1984), 114.

43. Serres, 69.

44. Teresa de Lauretis, *Alice Doesn't: Feminism, Semiotics, Cinema* (Bloomington: Indiana University Press, 1984), 157.

45. Gertude Koch, "Why Women Go to Men's Films," in Gisela Ecker, ed., *Feminist Aesthetics* (Boston: Beacon Press, 1985), 144–45.

46. "Comme, dans une apothéose de théâtre, un plissement de la robe de la fée, un tremblement de son petit doigt, dénoncent la présence matérielle d'une actrice vivante, là où nous étions incertains si nous n'avions pas devant les yeux une simple projection lumineuse." Marcel Proust, *A La Recherche du temps perdu*, 3 vols. (Paris: Gallimard Pléiade Edition, 1954), vol. 1, 175. The translation is by C. K. Scott Moncrieff. See Marcel Proust, *Swann's Way* ([1923] London: Chatto & Windus, 1973), 241.

47. Annette Kuhn, *The Power of the Image: Essays on Representation and Sexuality*, (London: Routledge & Kegan Paul, 1985), 10.

48. Siegfried Kracauer, *Theory of Film. The Redemption of Physical Reality* (New

York: Oxford University Press, 1960). The relevant passages read: "Struck by the reality character of the resultant images, the spectator cannot help reacting to them as he would to the material aspects of nature in the raw which these photographic images reproduce. . . . It is as if they urged him through their sheer presence unthinkingly to assimilate their indeterminate and often amorphous patterns. . . . The film renders the world in motion . . . the sight of it seems to have a 'resonance effect,' provoking in the spectator such kinesthetic responses as muscular reflexes, motor impulses, or the like. In any case, objective movement acts as a physiological stimulus" (158).

49. I am indebted to Morgan Ryan, who was my student at Duke University in 1982, for the original concept of "tactile communication" in film. Ryan suggests that these shots constitute a "visual carving" of reality, a term that has an affinity with Kracauer's "resonance effect."

CONCLUSION

1. Philippe Sollers, *Writing and the Experience of Limits*, ed. David Hayman and trans. Philip Barnard with David Hayman (New York: Columbia, 1983), 200.

2. Norine Voss, " 'Saying the Unsayable': An Introduction to Women's Autobiography," in Judith Specter, ed., *Gender Studies: New Directions in Feminist Criticism* (Bowling Green, Ohio: Bowling Green State University Popular Press, 1986), 218–33.

3. Gertrud Koch, "Why Women Go to Men's Films," in Gisela Ecker, ed., *Feminist Aesthetics* (Boston: Beacon Press, 1985), 112.

4. Mark Gerzon, *A Choice of Heroes* (Boston: Houghton Mifflin, 1982).

5. Silvia Bovenshen, "Is There a Feminist Aesthetic?" in *Feminist Aesthetic*, 39.

6. Judith Fetterley, *The Resisting Reader* (Bloomington: Indiana University Press, 1978), xxii.

7. On this point, see the discussion between Helen Fehervary, Claudia Lenssen, and Judith Mayne, "From Hitler to Hepburn: A Discussion of Women's Film Production and Reception," *New German Critique* 24–5 (1981–2): 172–85. As this book went to press, I became aware of Elfi Mikesch's and Monika Treut's *The Virgin Machine* (1988), a film that answers to many of the points I am raising here. Dorotee, an East German journalist who travels to the United States to research a story on romantic love, is permitted the full exploration of the film's diegetic space. In San Francisco she falls victim to Ramona, the star of a "for women only" strip show, who performs in male drag. The strip scene wittily complicates cinematic voyeurism by showing the performer's playful oscillation between her male impersonation and her female persona, and by portraying the reactions of the women spectators. The tryst between Ramona and Dorotee ends badly, as Ramona demands payment for the night they have spent together. The sexual politics of the "bachelor machine" is thus extended beyond its traditional heterosexual confines. On this topic, see also Celeste Fraser, "No Faking: New Feminist Works on Spectatorship, Pleasure, and the Female Body," *The Independent* 13.6 (1990): 26–30.

8. Teresa de Lauretis, *Technologies of Gender* (Bloomington: Indiana University Press, 1987), 138–39. See also Mary Crawford and Roger Chaffin, "Cognitive Research on Gender and Comprehension," in Elizabeth A. Flynn and Patrocinio P. Schweickart, eds., *Gender and Reading* (Baltimore: The Johns Hopkins University Press, 1986), 3–30.

9. Joanne S. Frye, *Living Stories, Telling Lives: Women and the Novel of Contemporary Experience* (Ann Arbor: University of Michigan Press, 1986), 197–98.

10. Stephen Heath, *Questions of Cinema* (Bloomington: Indiana University Press, 1981), 64.

Index

Individual films are listed under the director's name if the director is mentioned in the text. Foreign language titles are listed in their original language, followed by English language distribution titles, if any.